Editorial Project Manager
Eric Migliaccio

Editor in Chief
Karen J. Goldfluss, M.S. Ed.

Creative Director
Sarah M. Fournier

Cover Artist
Diem Pascarella

Illustrator
Clint McKnight

Art Coordinator
Renée Mc Elwee

Imaging
Amanda R. Harter

Publisher
Mary D. Smith, M.S. Ed.

MASTERING COMP

TCR 8063

Using Mu Reading Sources

Includes:

- 28 Units with 3 – 5 related text sources in a variety of genres and formats

- Multiple question types that promote higher-order thinking skills

- Open-ended response opportunities to encourage close reading

- Correlated to the Common Core State Standards

Teacher Created Resources

Author
Karen McRae

For correlations to the Common Core State Standards, see pages 109–112 of this book or visit *http://www.teachercreated.com/standards/*.

Teacher Created Resources
6421 Industry Way
Westminster, CA 92683
www.teachercreated.com

ISBN: 978-1-4206-8063-8

© 2015 Teacher Created Resources
Made in U.S.A.

Teacher Created Resources

Table of Contents

Introduction 2

How to Use This Book 4

Multiple-Source Units

1. Aaron's Errands 6

2. The Naming of the Storm 9

3. Written Without Ease 12

4. An Eponymous Comet 16

5. #34 for 34 19

6. Many Ways to Convey 22

7. At the Top, Looking Down 26

8. In the Blink of an Eye 29

9. The Fourth Time's the Charm 32

10. February 29, 2100 36

11. Baking Badly 39

12. The Winning Whiskers 42

13. Friggatriskaidekaphobia! 46

14. Everything Floats 49

15. Just Deserts 52

16. The Unneeded Earmuffs 56

17. A Fallible Friend 59

18. Pioneers in Space 62

19. A Grain of Salt 66

20. Winning Isn't Everything 69

21. Two One-of-a-Kinds 72

22. Double the Fun! 76

23. The Pet-Store Thief 79

24. The Four Applicants 82

25. Making Money 86

26. *Mean*'s Many Meanings 90

27. Mr. Yee's Mysteries 93

28. Two Sets of Directions 96

Additional Activities 100

Answer Key 101

Common Core State Standards 109

Introduction

Here we are, teaching and learning at the beginning of a new era of educational standards: the Common Core Era. This new directive has ushered in a slew of educational guidelines that are somewhat familiar and yet entirely ambitious. While the Common Core State Standards for English Language Arts address many educational basics (reading comprehension, proficiency in the conventions of English grammar, the ability to express oneself both in writing and in speech), they also seek to define what it means to be a literate, resourceful, perceptive person in the 21st century. Ultimately, they aim to equip each student with the tools needed to be that kind of person.

Introduction (cont.)

With this new, ambitious focus comes the need for a new type of educational material—one that challenges and interests students while meeting the multifaceted criteria of the Common Core. There are a total of 28 units in *Mastering Complex Text Using Multiple Reading Sources*, and each one fits the bill. Here's how:

✳ The units in this book are both familiar and innovative.

They are familiar in that they pair reading passages with activities that test reading comprehension. They are innovative in how they accomplish this goal through the use of multiple text sources and multiple answer formats. These materials promote deeper understanding and thought processes by prompting students to analyze, synthesize, hypothesize, and empathize.

✳ The use of multiple reading sources promotes close reading.

Close reading is the underlying goal of the Common Core State Standards for English Language Arts. Close reading involves understanding not just the explicit content of a reading passage but also all of the nuances contained therein. A close reading of a text reveals all of the inferential and structural components of the content, while also illuminating the craft that went into the writing of it.

The Common Core State Standards suggest that the best way to foster close reading of informational text is through text complexity. It offers four factors needed to create a high level of text complexity—all four of which are achieved through this book's use of multiple reading sources:

Factor	Meaning
1. Levels of Purpose	The purpose of the text should be implicit, hidden, or obscured in some way.
2. Structure	Texts of high complexity tend to have complex, implicit, or unconventional structures.
3. Language Conventionality or Clarity	Texts should use domain-specific language and feature language that is figurative, ironic, ambiguous, or otherwise unfamiliar.
4. Knowledge Demands	Complex texts make assumptions that readers can use life experiences, cultural awareness, and content knowledge to supplement their understanding of a text.

✳ The activities prompt students to explore the reading material from all angles.

By completing the four different activities found in each unit, students will be able to display a broad understanding of the reading material. Each activity and question is designed to make students think about what they have read—everything from how it was written, to why it was written that way, to how its subject matter can be applied to their lives. They gain experience locating information, making inferences from it, and applying knowledge in a variety of ways.

The units in this book are supplemented by a comprehensive answer key (pages 101–108) and a full list of Common Core State Standards correlations (pages 109–112). And even more educational value can be mined from each unit's reading material with "Additional Activities" (page 100). Make copies of this page (one per student per unit) and have students follow the instructions.

How to Use This Book

This book is divided into 28 units, which do not need to be taught in any particular order. Each unit is either three or four pages in length and is composed of reading material (one or two pages) and activity pages (two or three pages):

Reading Material

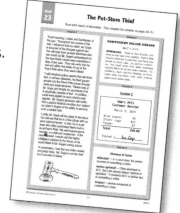

The reading material for each unit consists of three, four, or five text sources. Have students read all of a unit's text sources before proceeding to the activity pages. These sources complement each other, and a connective thread (or threads) runs throughout them. Sometimes these connections will be explicit, while at other times they will be hidden or obscured.

> ❄ **Another Approach** After reading the source material, ask students to name all of the ways in which the reading sources seem to be related or connected. See page 100 for more details.

Activity Pages

Each unit is supported by two or three pages of activities. These activity pages are divided into four parts:

Part 1

Standard RI.5.7 of the Common Core (from the **Integration of Knowledge and Ideas** section of the **Reading: Informational Text** strand) requires students to "draw on information from multiple print or digital sources, demonstrating the ability to locate an answer to a question quickly or to solve a problem efficiently." This section directly correlates to that standard. Students will gain valuable practice in scanning multiple text sources in order to locate information.

Before beginning this section, remind students to read the directions carefully. Some of the information can be found in two or more sources, which means that students will need to fill in more than one bubble in those instances.

> ❄ **Another Approach** Have your students practice their recognition of genres and formats. For each unit, have them fill in the chart on page 100.

Part 2

In this section, students are asked to provide the best answer(s) to multiple-choice questions. What sets these apart from the usual multiple-choice questions is their emphasis on higher-order thinking skills. Very few questions ask for simple recall of information. Instead, these questions are designed to provide practice and strengthen knowledge in a variety of areas, including the following:

❄ inference	❄ word etymology	❄ compare and contrast
❄ deduction	❄ parts of speech	❄ cause and effect
❄ grammar and usage	❄ literary devices	❄ analogies
❄ vocabulary in context	❄ authorial intent	❄ computation

> ❄ **Another Approach** Ask each student to write an original multiple-choice question based on the reading sources. Use the best or most interesting questions to create a student-generated quiz. See page 100 for more details.

How to Use This Book *(cont.)*

Activity Pages *(cont.)*

Part 3

This two-question section takes the skills addressed in Part 1 and approaches them from another angle. Part 3 is in the form of a scavenger hunt that asks students to search the sources in order to locate a word or phrase that fits the criteria described. Students are also asked to name the source in which they found the word or phrase.

> ✳ **Another Approach** Assign students to small groups, and have each group collaboratively come up with two suitable scavenger hunts from the reading material. These student-created scavenger hunts can then be completed and discussed by the entire class. See page 100 for more details.

Part 4

This section is composed of three questions that ask students to integrate information from several texts on the same topic in order to write knowledgeably about a subject. The vast majority of these questions are open-ended, while the rest involve using a new format (e.g., chart, diagram, graph) to organize and/or interpret data and information.

The questions in this section challenge students to blend close-reading concepts with flexible-thinking skills. Students are asked to do the following:

Analyze	Synthesize	Hypothesize	Empathize
✳ authorial choices ✳ intent of characters/ historical figures ✳ overall meanings ✳ quotations in context ✳ statistical data	✳ combine different takes on the same subject ✳ use information from different genres and formats (nonfiction, fiction, graphs, etc.) to draw conclusions ✳ compare and contrast characters, ideas, and concepts ✳ draw conclusions from information and/or numerical data	✳ make predictions about future events ✳ explore alternatives to previous choices	✳ connect to one's own life ✳ put oneself in a character's/ historical figure's place

> ✳ **Another Approach** The Common Core places a strong emphasis on teaching and applying speaking and listening skills. Many of the questions in Part 4 lend themselves well to meeting standards from this strand. Have individual students present oral reports on specific Part 4 questions. Or, form groups of students and ask them to engage in collaborative discussion before presenting their findings.

Aaron's Errands

Read each source below. Then complete the activities on pages 7–8.

Source 1

Dear Aaron,

Good morning! When I left for work, you were sleeping like a log. Now that you're awake, I need help! It's already the 9th of June. Your sister's birthday party is tomorrow! Dad is picking up the cake on his way home from work, and I'll put together all the party favors for Ariel's little friends when I get home. I'm worried there's too much to do and too little time to do it in. Can you please run a few errands for me?

I need you to drive to Foodland to pick up some groceries. The list is in the usual place on the fridge. But before you do that, I need you to go to the party store that's right next door to Foodland. I'll try to be really specific, but you may need to look around to see what they have. Remember, the party will have an "Under the Sea" theme.

Please get 2 packages each of plates, cups, and bowls. If they have mermaid ones, get those. If not, blue would be fine. Also, get some blue and green balloons and streamers. Anything I'm forgetting?

Thanks so much, Aaron. You're a big help! Your sis will appreciate you!

Love, Mom

Oh, two more things!
1. Take a $100 bill from the "secret" jar. That should be enough for everything.
2. Please save the receipts from both stores.

Source 2

Stuff to buy at Foodland
(for Ariel's b-day party!)

ice (2 bags)   juice boxes   soda (3 bottles)

water (lots!)   chips/pretzels candy

ice cream   fruit/melon

Source 3

PARTY WORLD
6/9/17   2:00 p.m.

2 pkg cups—blue	$6.00
2 pkg plates—mermaid	$8.00
2 pkg bowls—mermaid	$7.00
2 pkg napkins—blue	$4.00
bday candles—blue	$2.00
"Under the Sea" balloons	$5.00
streamers—green	$1.50
streamers—blue	$1.50
Subtotal	$35.00
Tax	$2.89
Total	**$37.89**

Source 4

Foodland
Friday, June 9, 2017   1:13 p.m.

watermelon whole	$4.99
red grapes 2.17 lbs.	$5.64
pineapple whole	$3.99
ice cream	$4.00
potato chips	$1.99
color candies	$2.50
juice bxs (case)	$5.99
soda	$1.33
soda	$1.33
soda	$1.33
goldfish crackers	$2.00
pretz twists	$1.50
ice (2 bags)	$5.00
btl water (2 cases)	$12.00
Subtotal	$53.59
Tax	$4.42
Total	**$58.01**

6

Aaron's Errands *(cont.)*

Name: _____

Part 1: Read each idea. Which source gives you this information? Fill in the correct bubble for each source. (Note: More than one bubble may be filled in for each idea.)

Information	Sources ➡	1	2	3	4
1. Aaron's family is having a party for Ariel.		○	○	○	○
2. Ariel's family shops at Foodland.		○	○	○	○
3. Party World is next to Foodland.		○	○	○	○
4. Party World sells party decorations.		○	○	○	○

Part 2: Fill in the bubble(s) next to the best answer(s) to each question.

5. Which two items that Aaron bought were **not** mentioned in either the note or the grocery list?

Ⓐ watermelon   Ⓒ napkins

Ⓑ crackers   Ⓓ candy

6. Which of these words from the sources is **not** an abbreviated form of a longer word?

Ⓐ fridge   Ⓒ b-day

Ⓑ mermaid   Ⓓ sis

7. Which answer gives the **most specific** information about when Ariel's birthday party is scheduled to occur?

Ⓐ Saturday, June 10   Ⓒ Saturday, June 10, 2017

Ⓑ Friday, June 9, 2017   Ⓓ Saturday, June 9, 2:00 p.m.

8. Which of these would **not** be considered an errand?

Ⓐ making party favors for Ariel's birthday party

Ⓑ picking up the cake for Ariel's birthday party

Ⓒ buying food for Ariel's birthday party

Ⓓ buying decorations for Ariel's birthday party

Part 3: Search "Aaron's Errands" to find one example of each of the following. Then write the number of the source in which you located this information.

9. a simile _____ Source #: _____

10. a possessive noun _____ Source #: _____

Name: _____

Part 4: Refer back to the sources, and use complete sentences to answer these questions.

11. Was $100 enough to buy everything from both stores? _____

In the box below, show each mathematical step you used to determine the answer. Also show how much more money was needed or how much money was left over.

(answer box)

12. Do you think Aaron is Ariel's younger or older brother? How can you infer this answer from the information given? Use at least three pieces of information from the sources as evidence.

_____

_____

_____

_____

_____

13. Did Aaron follow his mother's instruction to go to the party store before Foodland? _____

Cite evidence from the sources to show how you got your answer.

_____

_____

_____

_____

_____

Bonus: Why might Aaron's mother have asked him to go to the stores in that specific order?

_____

_____

The Naming of the Storm

Read each source below. Then complete the activities on pages 10–11.

Source 1

Dear Diary,

I can't believe it. Our whole town is bracing for one of the worst hurricanes in history. It is swirling over the Atlantic Ocean and heading toward our state. The threat of a big storm seems to rear its ugly head every year during hurricane season, but this is different. This storm is personal. It has my name!

All around our town, I hear cries of "Hurricane Sara is coming! Board up your windows. Prepare to evacuate. Get out of town before Sara hits. Sara is the worst thing ever!" It is as if the whole town has my name on their minds, and they are not thinking happy thoughts. I really hope that this whole Hurricane Sara thing just blows over and goes away. I want my good name back!

Signed,
You Know Who

Source 2

Some Devastating Hurricanes of the 21st Century

Name	Month/Year	Deaths*	Damages*
Charley	August 2004	35	$15 billion
Ivan	September 2004	124	$23 billion
Katrina	August 2005	1,836	$108 billion
Stan	October 2005	1,668	$4 billion
Ike	September 2008	195	$37 billion
Sandy	October 2012	286	$68 billion

* Figures may differ according to various sources.

Source 3

I work at the National Hurricane Center (NHC) in Miami, Florida. One thing we do there is track storms. If a storm is really big — that is, if it contains winds of 40 miles per hour or greater — then we name it. In fact, there's a whole policy dedicated to the naming of these big storms.

There are six lists of 21 names each that we use. We alternate these lists every six years. So, for instance, the list that was used in 2000 was also used in 2006, 2012, etc.

Each name on a list starts with a different letter of the alphabet (though we don't use names starting with Q, U, X, Y, or Z). We go in alphabetical order, so that means that the first major storm of the season gets the name that begins with "A" (for example, the first major storm of 2010 was called Hurricane Alex). We use the same list of names every six years. Some names do get retired, however. If a storm that's been given a name turns out to be particularly devastating, we won't use that name ever again. For example, Hurricane Rita caused $12 billion worth of damages and killed 62 people in September of 2005. Consequently, there will never be another storm named Rita. That name is replaced by another name that begins with "R."

Part 1: Read each idea. Which source gives you this information? Fill in the correct bubble for each source. (Note: More than one bubble may be filled in for each idea.)

Information	Sources ➡	1	2	3
1. The NHC is located in Florida.		○	○	○
2. Storms can cause over $10 billion in damages.		○	○	○
3. Large storms are given people's names.		○	○	○
4. A storm name can be retired.		○	○	○

Part 2: Fill in the bubble next to the best answer to each question.

5. What is the name of the narrator in Source 1?

    Ⓐ Rita   Ⓑ Katrina   Ⓒ Sandy   Ⓓ Sara

6. What happens when a storm name is retired?

    Ⓐ It is erased from the history books.

    Ⓑ It is never used again.

    Ⓒ It is only given to another big storm.

    Ⓓ That letter is no longer used for storm names.

7. When the narrator in Source 1 says the threat of a storm seems to "rear its ugly head" every year, which literary device is she using?

    Ⓐ simile   Ⓒ onomatopoeia

    Ⓑ alliteration   Ⓓ personification

8. If a storm with winds over 40 mph hits in the year 2030, which of these could be its name?

    Ⓐ Hurricane Oscar   Ⓒ Hurricane Sandy

    Ⓑ Hurricane Zelda   Ⓓ Hurricane Xavier

Part 3: Search "The Naming of the Storm" to find one example of each of the following. Then write the number of the source in which you located this information.

9. a word with five syllables _____ Source #: _____

10. a word meaning "to leave a place of danger" _____ Source #: _____

The Naming of the Storm *(cont.)*

Name: _____

Part 4: Refer back to the sources, and use complete sentences to answer these questions.

11. Using the information you have read, what time of year seems to be "hurricane season"? Shade in the box of the time period below, and then cite examples from your sources to back up your claim.

early summer	late summer	early spring	middle of winter

_____

_____

_____

_____

12. Imagine that you are like the narrator from Source 1, and a storm with your name is predicted to be a powerful hurricane. How would you feel? Would you be excited or worried? Would you wish that the storm had a different name? Explain your feelings.

_____

_____

_____

_____

_____

_____

13. Imagine the National Hurricane Center needs to come up with a whole new list of storm names for the coming year, and they have put you in charge. Be creative as you create your list of 21 names. (Note: You must use the rules set forth in Source 3.)

_____ _____ _____

_____ _____ _____

_____ _____ _____

_____ _____ _____

_____ _____ _____

_____ _____ _____

_____ _____ _____

Written Without Ease

Read each source below. Then complete the activities on pages 13–15.

Source 1

The novel *Gadsby* was written by Ernest Vincent Wright and published in 1939. It tells the story of its title character, an ambitious man named John Gadsby. He lives in a fictional American town called Branton Hills. This town is in decline, and the novel's protagonist decides to do something about it. *Gadsby* becomes mayor, and the town thrives.

That is the plot of *Gadsby*, but it is not what makes this novel really unique and ambitious. What makes *Gadsby* special is that it is written without the help of one very important thing: the letter *e*. There are over 50,000 words in *Gadsby*, and not one contains the letter *e*. This must have been difficult considering the letter *e* appears in about 12.5% of the words in the English language. It was so difficult in fact that as he typed the final manuscript, Wright tied down the letter *e* on his typewriter so that "none of that vowel might slip in, accidentally."

So what drove this author to attempt such a feat? In the introduction to *Gadsby*, Wright said he was tired of hearing people say, "It can't be done."

Source 2

Roots

(from the Greek language)

homo- means "same"

lipo- means "missing"

-gram means "something written"

-phone means "sound"

Source 3

The following chart shows the frequency with which each letter appears in words in the English language. Each percentage has been rounded to the nearest 0.5% (except for letters appearing in fewer than 0.5% of words).

Most Common Letters in English	
A	8%
B	1.5%
C	3%
D	4.5%
E	12.5%
F	2%
G	2%
H	6%
I	7%
J	0.15%
K	1%
L	4%
M	2.5%
N	6.5%
O	7.5%
P	2%
Q	0.09%
R	6%
S	6.5%
T	9%
U	3%
V	1%
W	2.5%
X	0.15%
Y	2%
Z	0.07%

Written Without Ease (cont.)

Name: _____

Part 1: Read each idea. Which source gives you this information? Fill in the correct bubble for each source. (Note: More than one bubble may be filled in for each idea.)

Information	Sources ➡	1	2	3
1. The letter *e* is in about 12.5% of words in English.		○	○	○
2. Wright tied down the *e* key while typing *Gadsby*.		○	○	○
3. The root *-phone* means "sound."		○	○	○
4. The most commonly used letter in English is *e*.		○	○	○

Part 2: Fill in the bubble next to the best answer to each question.

5. Which is **not** true of John Gadsby?

Ⓐ He is the author of *Gadsby*.
Ⓑ He is the title character of *Gadsby*.
Ⓒ He is the protagonist of *Gadsby*.
Ⓓ He is the mayor of Branton Hills.

6. According to Source 3, what are the five most common letters in the English language? They must be in the correct order from one (most common) to five.

Ⓐ E, A, I, O, U
Ⓑ E, T, S, A, I
Ⓒ E, T, A, O, I
Ⓓ E, A, T, I, O

7. Which of these does not contain the letter *e*?

Ⓐ "What is missing in the book called *Gadsby*?"
Ⓑ "*Gadsby* is an ambitious book about an ambitious man."
Ⓒ "All who pick up *Gadsby* will find it worthwhile."
Ⓓ "John Gadsby is the protagonist of *Gadsby*."

8. There is a word that combines two Greek roots and means "to leave out a letter." What is this word, which could be used to describe a piece of writing like *Gadsby*?

Ⓐ a lipophone
Ⓑ a homogram
Ⓒ a lipogram
Ⓓ a homophone

Part 3: Search "Writing Without Ease" to find one example of each of the following. Then write the number of the source in which you located this information.

9. the name of an occupation _____ Source #: _____

10. a proper adjective _____ Source #: _____

Written Without Ease (cont.)

Name: _____

Part 4: Refer back to the sources, and use complete sentences to answer these questions.

11. From Source 2, we can see that the word *homophone* means "same sound." Homophones are words that have the same sound but have different spellings and different meanings. Here are a few examples:

bear and **bare**   **see** and **sea**   **their, there,** and **they're**

What homophone could be substituted for one of the words in the title "Written Without Ease"? Explain your answer. How is the title appropriate with either homophone?

_____

_____

_____

_____

_____

12. Can you write an entire paragraph without ever using one letter? Give it a try. Choose one of the vowels below. Cross it out. Then write a paragraph that does not contain that letter. You can write about any subject you choose.

A   E   I   O   U

_____

_____

_____

_____

_____

_____

_____

_____

_____

_____

Written Without Ease (cont.)

Name: _____

Part 4 (cont.):

13. Complete the bar graph. The first bar has been shaded for you. Then answer the question below.

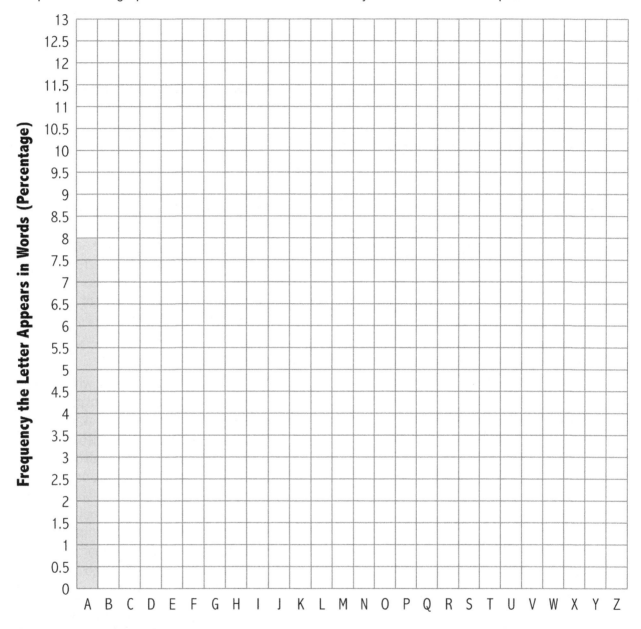

Question: Which of the data surprised you? Did you think a particular letter would appear more frequently or less frequently? Choose one letter, and explain why its frequency is surprising to you.

_____

_____

_____

_____

An Eponymous Comet

Read each source below. Then complete the activities on pages 17–18.

Source 1

Edmond Halley
English astronomer

Born: November 8, 1656

Died: January 14, 1742

Best Known For: Computing the orbit of (and lending his name to) a comet that can be seen from Earth every 75–76 years

Source 2

Comets are chunks of ice, dust, and rock that move through space. Some comets are **periodic**, which means they make regular passes by Earth. One such comet is called Halley's Comet, and it can be observed from Earth every 75 years or so. The following list shows the years since 1500 in which the comet could be observed from Earth. The exact dates given show when the comet came the closest to the Sun in its orbit.

August 26, 1531
October 27, 1607
September 15, 1682
March 13, 1759
November 16, 1835
April 20, 1910
February 9, 1986
July 28, 2061*

* predicted date

Source 3

eponym
noun

an object, discovery, invention, place, etc., derived from the proper name of a person

examples: Achilles' heel, Newton's law, Pasteurized milk, Halley's comet

other form(s): **eponymous** (adjective)

Source 4

A bell rang, like it did every weekday at 8:00 in the morning, and Ellie's computer screen went green. Today's date and the current time flashed across the screen. Then Mr. Clock appeared. He was wearing a silver suit and standing in front of a large wall filled with live video images of our solar system. In an excited voice, he began his morning lecture.

"Good morning, everyone. Well, what an eventful evening we had last night! Something for which we've been waiting our entire lifetimes finally happened. Halley's Comet reached its *perihelion*. This word comes from the Greek *peri*, meaning 'around,' and *helios*, meaning 'sun.' Last night, the orbiting comet came as close to the Sun as it will until the year 2137, when this eponymous comet is due to return. So I hope you got a good look at this long-awaited event!"

An Eponymous Comet (cont.)

Name: _____

Part 1: Read each idea. Which source gives you this information? Fill in the correct bubble for each source. (Note: More than one bubble may be filled in for each idea.)

Information	Sources ➡	1	2	3	4
1. The word *perihelion* is Greek in origin.		○	○	○	○
2. The term "Achilles' heel" is an eponym.		○	○	○	○
3. Halley's Comet will next be seen in the year 2061.		○	○	○	○
4. Halley's Comet is named after a person.		○	○	○	○

Part 2: Fill in the bubble next to the best answer to each question.

5. How many times could Halley's Comet be observed from Earth during Edmond Halley's lifetime?

Ⓐ 1

Ⓑ 2

Ⓒ 4

Ⓓ 7

6. In Source 4, the date and time flashes on Ellie's computer screen. Using the information given throughout the sources, what flashed on Ellie's screen?

Ⓐ July 29, 2061 8:00 PM

Ⓑ July 29, 2016 8:00 PM

Ⓒ July 29, 1986 8:00 AM

Ⓓ July 29, 2061 8:00 AM

7. Using information given in Source 3, who can you infer developed the process of using heat to make milk safer to drink?

Ⓐ Achilles

Ⓑ Isaac Newton

Ⓒ Louis Pasteur

Ⓓ Edmund Halley

8. Which 18th-century date shows when Halley's Comet reached its perihelion?

Ⓐ March 13, 1759

Ⓑ November 16, 1759

Ⓒ November 16, 1835

Ⓓ April 20, 1835

Part 3: Search "An Eponymous Comet" to find one example of each of the following. Then write the number of the source in which you located this information.

9. the name of a part of speech _____   Source #: _____

10. the name of a color _____   Source #: _____

Part 4: Refer back to the sources, and use complete sentences to answer these questions.

11. Mark Twain is the famous author of *Adventures of Huckleberry Finn*. He was born on November 30, 1835, and he died on April 21, 1910. In 1909, he was quoted as saying, "I came in with Halley's Comet in 1835. It is coming again next year, and I expect to go out with it." What does he mean when he says he "came in" with the comet? Was he correct when he predicted that he would "go out with it" the next year? Give details in your answer.

_____

_____

_____

_____

_____

12. How does the title "An Eponymous Comet" relate to Halley's Comet? Give examples from at least two sources to support your reasoning.

_____

_____

_____

_____

_____

13. How old will you be when Halley's Comet is at its next perihelion? Give your answer in years and months (example, "55 years, 7 months").

Do you think you'll want to see Halley's Comet? Why or why not?

_____

_____

_____

_____

#34 for 34

Read each source below. Then complete the activities on pages 20–21.

Source 1

Four lifelong friends sat and talked about the best athletes they had ever seen. Carl had just stated his case for Muhammad Ali being the greatest.

"What a boxer," agreed Joe. "Lightning-quick and as graceful as a ballerina."

Stu shook his head. "Babe Ruth. That's the answer. The Babe swatted over 700 home runs."

Joe nodded and said, "He'll always be remembered as one of the greats."

Paul piped in, "It's got to be Usain Bolt. He's the fastest man alive. Bolt broke three world records at the 2008 Olympic Games."

"These are all great athletes," said Joe. "I'll tell you what, though: the greatest one I ever saw was Bo Jackson."

"What? Really?" exclaimed the guys.

"He excelled at two different pro sports at the same time!" said Joe. "As a baseball player, he hit towering home runs and made diving catches in the outfield. He once ran up the outfield wall after making a catch. How does a 250-pound human do that?"

Carl reminisced, "I once saw him break a bat over his knee like it was a toothpick."

"He really shined as a football player," continued Joe. "What a combination of power and speed! As a running back, he could outrun most defenders, or he could bull right through them if he had to."

"How many football games did Bo play?" protested Paul. "Not enough to be called 'the greatest'."

Joe nodded, "His athletic success was short-lived, but only because he suffered such a terrible injury. I can still remember that playoff game when he got hurt. It was January of 1991. He had just been tackled after a beautiful 34-yard run. His left hip took the full force of his body as he went to the ground. That was the last time Bo carried a football in a game."

Stu shook his head, "It's a shame. No one knows how great he could have been."

Source 2

Baseball Player (Years Played)	Total Home Runs	
Babe Ruth (1914–1935)		714
Bo Jackson (1986–1994)		141

Source 3

Bo Jackson

RB • #34

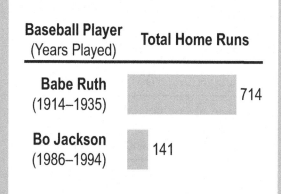

Born: November 30, 1962

Height: 6'1

Weight: 227 lbs.

Jersey #: 34

Position: Running Back

Rushing Statistics

Year	Team	Games	Yards	Touchdowns
1987	Los Angeles Raiders	7	554	4
1988	Los Angeles Raiders	10	580	3
1989	Los Angeles Raiders	11	950	4
1990	Los Angeles Raiders	10	698	5
1991*	Los Angeles Raiders	1	77	0
Career		39	2859	16

playoff game

#34 for 34 *(cont.)*

Name: _____

Part 1: Read each idea. Which source gives you this information? Fill in the correct bubble for each source. (Note: More than one bubble may be filled in for each idea.)

Information Sources ➡	1	2	3
1. Babe Ruth hit over 700 home runs.	○	○	○
2. Bo Jackson played the outfield in baseball.	○	○	○
3. Bo Jackson was a running back in football.	○	○	○
4. Bo Jackson ran for over 900 yards in 1989.	○	○	○

Part 2: Fill in the bubble next to the best answer to each question.

5. Which statement is the most accurate?

 Ⓐ Babe Ruth hit about twice as many home runs as Bo Jackson.

 Ⓑ Babe Ruth hit about three times as many home runs as Bo Jackson.

 Ⓒ Babe Ruth hit about four times as many home runs as Bo Jackson.

 Ⓓ Babe Ruth hit about five times as many home runs as Bo Jackson.

6. In Source 1, Paul asks, "How many football games did Bo play?" What is the answer to that question?

 Ⓐ 16   Ⓒ 141

 Ⓑ 39   Ⓓ 227

7. Which of these word pairs from Source 1 are not synonyms?

 Ⓐ *hit* and *swatted*   Ⓒ *lifelong* and *short-lived*

 Ⓑ *running* and *rushing*   Ⓓ *remembered* and *reminisced*

8. The following pairings match the name of an athlete with something he was known for doing. Which of these matches is not correct?

 Ⓐ Ali, graceful boxer   Ⓒ Ruth, leaping catches

 Ⓑ Jackson, played two sports   Ⓓ Bolt, fastest person

Part 3: Search "#34 for 34" to find one example of each of the following. Then write the number of the source in which you located this information.

 9. an abbreviation _____ Source #: _____

 10. a simile _____ Source #: _____

#34 for 34 (cont.)

Name: _____

Part 4: Refer back to the sources, and use complete sentences to answer these questions.

11. When people are trying to convince others, they sometimes use exaggeration to make their case sound even better than it is. Circle the exaggeration below from Source 1. Explain why you chose that one.

"How does a 250-pound human do that?"   **"The Babe swatted over 700 home runs."**   **"Bolt broke three world records at the 2008 Olympic Games."**

_____

_____

_____

_____

12. What could the title "#34 for 34" refer to? Tell what each "34" stands for, and provide evidence from at least two sources to show how you know this.

_____

_____

_____

_____

_____

_____

13. Can an athlete who only competed for a short period of time be considered one of the best of all time? Take a stance and give reasons to support the position you have chosen. (There are no right or wrong answers!)

_____

_____

_____

_____

_____

_____

Many Ways to Convey

Read each source below. Then complete the activities on pages 23–25.

Source 1

Nick and his dad set a bowl of water on the driveway. The stray cat cautiously approached the bowl. She looked thin, and she had some scratches on her ears and neck. Slowly, the cat began to lap at the water. Nick reached out to pet the cat, but his father stopped him.

The cat jerked her head up and stared at Nick. Her ears flattened back, and the hair on her back stood up.

"What's she doing?" whispered Nick.

"I think she's conveying a message," said Nick's father. "She can't use words, so she's using body language to say, 'Please stay away. I don't want to be petted.'"

Source 2

Time Travel Is Possible!

Money Needed: $13 million

Raised So Far: $4,200

Who wouldn't want to visit the future or relive the past? Well, it's now almost possible! I can build a time machine that works. I just need a little cash to build the prototype. This will be a model from which other machines can be built. And if you donate as little as $1,000, I will credit that amount toward the purchase of your very own machine! Imagine owning a conveyance that can transport you into the past or future . . . all from the convenience of your home!

Please e-mail me for more details. This offer won't last long.

Source 3

Reviewer: Jeremy Jones

Restaurant: Pizza-Go-Round

Rating: ★★★★☆

As I walked into this restaurant, I thought, "Did I just time-travel to the year 2080?" There were slices of pizza moving all around the place! The food was serving itself!

"How is that possible?" you ask. Here's how: a system of conveyor belts winds throughout the restaurant. The chefs set plates of piping-hot pizza on these moving belts, so the plates pass right in front of you. If you see something that looks good, just grab it. They know how much to charge you by the number and shapes of the plates you take. The round plates have slices of plain cheese pizza. Those are $1.50 each. The oval plates have pizza with toppings, like pepperoni. Those are $2.50. The slices on the square plates are fancier, so they're $4.00 each. I had one with steak on it. Yum! I filled up on pizza for $10.50. I can live with that.

I was all set to give this place five stars for inventing a whole new way to feed me, but then my friend said that these kinds of restaurants have been around for a long time. I looked it up on my phone, and she's right! The first one opened in 1958 in Osaka, Japan. It seems that a lot of restaurants use conveyor belts to serve sushi, which I know is raw fish. No, thanks, I'll stick with pizza!

Many Ways to Convey (cont.)

Name: _____

Part 1: A form of the word *convey* is used and underlined in each of the sources on page 22. Notice how it is used each time. Then fill in the correct bubble to match the usage of the word with the correct source.

Information	Sources ➡	1	2	3
1. A form of the word *convey* is used as an adjective.		○	○	○
2. A form of the word *convey* is used as a noun.		○	○	○
3. A form of the word *convey* is used as a verb.		○	○	○

Part 2: Fill in the bubble next to the best answer to each question.

4. What seems to be the main reason why the reviewer in Source 3 does not give the restaurant a five-star rating?

  Ⓐ He doesn't like the food.

  Ⓑ He finds out the idea isn't original.

  Ⓒ He thinks the pizza was too hot.

  Ⓓ He thinks the pizza is too expensive.

5. Which of these words is a synonym for *prototype*?

  Ⓐ intention   Ⓑ system   Ⓒ transport   Ⓓ model

6. In Source 1, which of these reasons is one we **cannot** infer for why the cat wants Nick and his dad to stay away?

  Ⓐ She has been in a fight recently.

  Ⓑ She feels threatened by them.

  Ⓒ She is worried they might take the water away.

  Ⓓ She does not like the taste of water.

7. For Source 2, which of these best describes the author's intent?

  Ⓐ to tell a story to readers

  Ⓑ to persuade readers to do something

  Ⓒ to review a product that readers can buy

  Ⓓ to inform readers about the science of time travel

8. In Source 3, the reviewer writes, "I can live with that." What would be another way the reviewer could have phrased his/her opinion?

  Ⓐ "That is an acceptable amount to pay."

  Ⓑ "I wanted more, but I couldn't afford to buy it."

  Ⓒ "At least I didn't have to tip a waiter."

  Ⓓ "That is what pizza costs everywhere else."

Part 3: Search "Many Ways to Convey" to find one example of each of the following. Then write the number of the source in which you located this information.

9. a hyphenated word used as a verb _____ Source #: _____

10. a hyphenated word used as an adjective _____ Source #: _____

Many Ways to Convey (cont.)

Name: _____

Part 4: Refer back to the sources, and use complete sentences to answer these questions.

11. Look at the picture below. It shows an overhead view of a conveyor belt at the Pizza-Go-Round restaurant. Using the information from Source 3, complete the chart to show how much each slice of pizza costs. Then calculate the total cost.

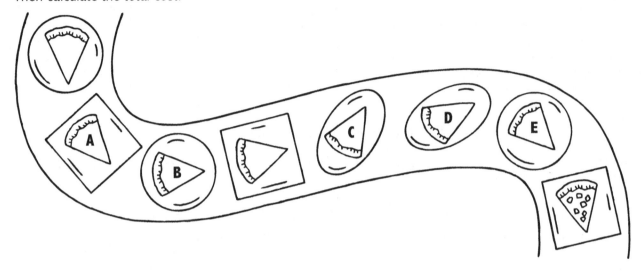

	Slice A	Slice B	Slice C	Slice D	Slice E	Total Cost
Cost Per Slice	+	+	+	+		

12. Think about how the different forms of the word *convey* are used in "Many Ways to Convey"—from the conveying of a message in Source 1 to the time-travel conveyance in Source 2 to the conveyor-belt restaurant in Source 3. What do all of these have in common? In your own words, provide one definition for the word *convey* that is based on how the word is used in all three sources. Then explain how you decided on this definition.

Definition: _____

_____

Explanation: _____

_____

_____

_____

_____

_____

_____

Name: _____

Part 4 *(cont.):*

13. Think about a restaurant you visited recently. What was the experience like? How was the food? In the form below, write a review of the restaurant. Give the restaurant a rating. Include as many details as possible to convey your opinion of the restaurant.

Name of Restaurant: _____

Date Visited: _____

Rating (fill in the number of stars): ☆ ☆ ☆ ☆ ☆

Your Review: _____

_____

_____

_____

_____

_____

_____

_____

_____

_____

_____

_____

_____

_____

_____

_____

_____

_____

_____

At the Top, Looking Down

Read each source below. Then complete the activities on pages 27–28.

Source 1

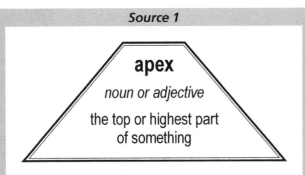

apex

noun or adjective

the top or highest part
of something

Source 2

Mr. Cross pointed to the chart on the whiteboard. It showed some animals, with arrows going from one animal to another. He explained, "All living things require energy to breathe, move around, and think. They even need energy to sleep. So where do most living things get energy?"

"From food?" guessed Greg.

"That's right," said Mr. Cross, "they get it from food. As animals, we eat plants or other animals. All animals do this. Plants, on the other hand, make their own food. They use the energy from the Sun to do this. Now look again at this chart. It shows a simple food chain. The arrows show the direction that energy travels. In other words, an arrow goes from the Sun to the plant, because the plant takes its energy (food) from the Sun. The arrow goes from the plant to the small animal, because this animal is an herbivore. It gets its energy by eating plants. The small mammal is then hunted and eaten by a larger animal. This continues all the way up to the top of the food chain. Up there, we find the lion, who is the king of this habitat. He has no natural predators other than himself. No one hunts him for food. Well, humans, of course, have been known to hunt lions, but that's another story."

Source 3

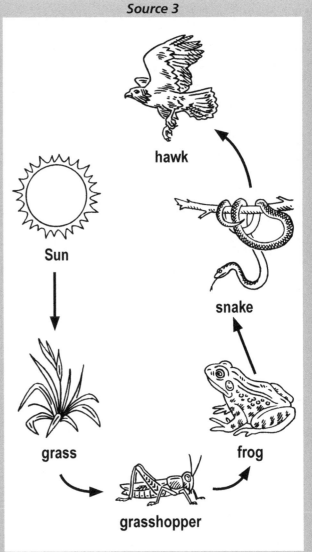

Sun

hawk

snake

grass

grasshopper

frog

Source 4

Habitat	Apex Predator
tall trees near water	bald eagle
swamps and rivers	American crocodile
oceans (moderate temperature)	great white shark
African grasslands	lion
oceans (cold temperatures)	killer whale (orca)

At the Top, Looking Down (cont.)

Name: _____

Part 1: Read each idea. Which source gives you this information? Fill in the correct bubble for each source. (Note: More than one bubble may be filled in for each idea.)

Information	Sources ➡	1	2	3	4
1. Hawks eat snakes, and snakes eat frogs.		○	○	○	○
2. We use energy when we think or sleep.		○	○	○	○
3. Lions are at the top of certain food chains.		○	○	○	○
4. The apex of a mountain would be its highest point.		○	○	○	○

Part 2: Fill in the bubble next to the best answer to each question.

5. Which source describes a food chain but does not show a diagram of one?

Ⓐ Source 1   Ⓑ Source 2   Ⓒ Source 3   Ⓓ Source 4

6. The temperatures in the ocean around Antarctica are often near or below freezing. Which apex predator most likely lives there?

Ⓐ eagle   Ⓑ orca   Ⓒ crocodile   Ⓓ great white shark

7. Which of these best summarizes Mr. Cross's speech to his class?

Ⓐ Living things need energy, which they get from the Sun and/or from food.

Ⓑ All living things are predators, which hunt food in order to get energy.

Ⓒ We need energy to do everything, even sleep.

Ⓓ In a food chain, the direction of the arrow shows where the energy goes.

8. In Source 2, when Mr. Cross says, "but that's another story," what does he most likely mean?

Ⓐ The hunting of lions by humans isn't appropriate to his lesson about food chains.

Ⓑ He has a personal story to tell about lions and humans interacting in the wild.

Ⓒ There are great fictional books about humans and lions that are worth reading.

Ⓓ He isn't an expert on the subject of hunting lions, so he won't talk about it.

Part 3: Search "At the Top, Looking Down" to find one example of each of the following. Then write the number of the source in which you located this information.

9. word meaning *plant-eater* _____   Source #: _____

10. synonym for the word *hunters* _____   Source #: _____

©*Teacher Created Resources*   27   *#8063 Mastering Complex Text*

Part 4: Refer back to the sources, and use complete sentences to answer these questions.

11. One of the headings on the chart of Source 4 is "Apex Predator." What can you infer is the meaning of this term? Use the information from the various sources to come up with your answer.

_____

_____

_____

_____

_____

_____

_____

12. Source 3 shows a food chain. A hawk is one part of that chain. There are two meanings for the title "At the Top, Looking Down" as it relates to the hawk. What are they?

_____

_____

_____

_____

_____

_____

_____

13. Would you say that humans are apex predators? Explain why or why not.

_____

_____

_____

_____

_____

_____

_____

In the Blink of an Eye

Read each source below. Then complete the activities on pages 30–31.

Source 1

statistics

noun

numerical data on a subject, the samples of which can be collected, analyzed, and interpreted

Source 2

Standing in front of a plastic model of a large eyeball, Professor Shorts asked, "Why do we blink our eyes?" The voices of his students hushed and then became altogether silent.

The professor continued, "We've known for a while that blinking serves a few purposes. For one, it provides moisture to the surface of your eyeball. Without this moisture, your eyeball will feel dried out. Your vision may suffer. Two, blinking actually cleans your eyeball. Tiny particles of dust and other foreign objects are constantly landing on the surface of your eye. As you blink, the up-and-down motion of your eyelids wipes these things away. These reasons for blinking are easily understood and observed. New research, however, hints that there may be another benefit we receive from blinking. This research shows that the focus center of our brains takes a tiny rest when we blink. It powers down for the briefest of moments. When we open our eyes again—which happens in mere milliseconds—our attention is refocused. In this way, the act of blinking is like a reset button for the brain."

Source 3

The Human Eye

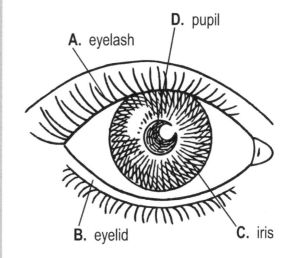

A. eyelash
D. pupil
B. eyelid
C. iris

Source 4

The following chart shows how often three different groups of people blink their eyes over certain periods of time.

Number of Minutes ➡	1	5	10	60
Average Person	15	75	150	900
Young Baby	2	10	20	120
Person Using Computer	7	35	70	420

In the Blink of an Eye _(cont.)_

Name: _____

Part 1: Read each idea. Which source gives you this information? Fill in the correct bubble for each source. (Note: More than one bubble may be filled in for each idea.)

Information	Sources ➡	1	2	3	4
1. On average, babies blink fewer times than adults.		○	○	○	○
2. Dust often lands on your eyeballs.		○	○	○	○
3. This source gives a definition of _statistics_.		○	○	○	○
4. This source gives an example of statistics.		○	○	○	○

Part 2: Fill in the bubble next to the best answer to each question.

5. Which of these describes a person who blinks the fewest times?

   Ⓐ a computer user in 10 minutes   Ⓒ the average person in 10 minutes

   Ⓑ a young baby in 40 minutes   Ⓓ the average person in 5 minutes

6. Professor Shorts says that "foreign objects" often land on the surface of the eye. What is the meaning of _foreign_ in this description?

   Ⓐ from another country   Ⓒ in an improper place

   Ⓑ not natural, alien   Ⓓ of a different language

7. When it comes to blinking, which labeled part in Source 3 most acts like a windshield wiper?

   Ⓐ A   Ⓒ C

   Ⓑ B   Ⓓ D

8. In Professor Shorts' description of brain activity during the act of blinking, to what does he seem to be comparing the brain?

   Ⓐ an eyeball   Ⓒ an electronic machine

   Ⓑ a scientist   Ⓓ a foreign object

Part 3: Search "In the Blink of an Eye" to find one example of each of the following. Then write the number of the source in which you located this information.

9. the smallest period of time mentioned _____ Source #: _____

10. a synonym for "shortest [amount of time]" _____ Source #: _____

In the Blink of an Eye *(cont.)*

Name: _____

Part 4: Refer back to the sources, and use complete sentences to answer these questions.

11. If you wanted to use the information in Source 4 to calculate how often the average person blinks in one week, how would you do that? Explain each step. (Note: You don't need to do the math. Just describe the process you would use to find the answer.)

_____

_____

_____

_____

_____

_____

12. In Source 2, the professor mentions three benefits that come from blinking. On the lines below, use your own words to quickly summarize each benefit.

❶ _____

_____

❷ _____

_____

❸ _____

_____

13. What can you infer are the effects of computer use on a person's eyeballs? Give reasons taken from more than one of the sources provided. Use statistics to strengthen your position.

_____

_____

_____

_____

_____

_____

_____

The Fourth Time's the Charm

Read each source below and on page 33. Then complete the activities on pages 34–35.

Source 1

RIO TO HOST 2016 GAMES

October 3, 2009 — Rio de Janeiro, Brazil, has been announced as the host city for the 2016 Summer Olympic Games. This will mark the first time the Games have been held on the continent of South America and only the third time they have been held in the Southern Hemisphere (Melbourne in 1956 and Sydney in 2000). The city of Rio de Janeiro had bid to host the Olympic Games on three previous occasions (1936, 2004, 2012) but had been passed over in each instance.

The Games of the XXXI Olympiad are scheduled to take place in August of 2016, when athletes from over 200 countries are expected to compete in over 300 events. As the host city, Rio de Janeiro will need to prepare the resources needed to accommodate hundreds of thousands of visitors over a two-week time period.

Source 2

In modern times, Roman numerals are still used in the naming of such things as Super Bowls, Olympiads, and copyright dates.

Roman numerals use symbols to represent numbers. For example . . .

I = 1   **V** = 5   **X** = 10

In most cases, symbols are placed from left to right in order of value.

VII = 7, because **V** = 5 and each **I** = 1 (5 + 1 + 1 = 7)

No more than three of the same symbol can be placed consecutively.

III is allowed, but **IIII** is not.

When a smaller value is placed before a larger value, the smaller value is subtracted from the larger value.

IV = 4, because **I** = 1 and **V** = 5 (5 – 1 = 4)

Source 3

What is an "Olympiad"?

As a sports blogger, I am frequently asked, "What is an Olympiad?" I have written my answer to this question twice before, but I still get asked this question! I will try one more time. As the saying goes, "The third time's the charm."

Many people think that "Olympiad" is just a fancy word for "Olympics." It's not, though it is definitely associated with the Games. The term "Olympiad" dates back to the time of the Ancient Greeks. It refers to a time period of four years. These days, an Olympiad begins on January 1 of the year the Summer Olympic Games are scheduled to be held, and it lasts for four calendar years. For example, the first modern Olympiad began on January 1, 1896, and ended on December 31, 1899.

More Info

▶ Olympiads are referred to by Roman numerals, so that the first modern Olympiad is actually referred to as the "I Olympiad." In 2012, the XXX Olympiad was held in London.

▶ Even if the Games are not held, the Olympiad is counted. As a result of such major events as World War I (1914–1918) and World War II (1939–1945), this has occurred three times since 1896.

The Fourth Time's the Charm *(cont.)*

This chart shows every city that has hosted the Summer Olympic Games in modern times.

The Host Cities

Year	Olympiad	Opening Ceremonies	Closing Ceremonies	Host City	Host Country
1896	I	April 6	April 15	Athens	Greece
1900	II	May 14	October 28	Paris	France
1904	III	July 1	November 23	St. Louis, MO	United States
1908	IV	April 27	October 31	London	England
1912	V	May 5	July 27	Stockholm	Sweden
1920	VII	April 20	September 12	Antwerp	Belgium
1924	VIII	May 4	July 27	Paris	France
1928	IX	July 28	August 12	Amsterdam	The Netherlands
1932	X	July 30	August 14	Los Angeles, CA	United States
1936	XI	August 1	August 16	Berlin	Germany
1948	XIV	July 29	August 14	London	England
1952	XV	July 19	August 3	Helsinki	Finland
1956	XVI	November 22	December 8	Melbourne	Australia
1960	XVII	August 25	September 11	Rome	Italy
1964	XVIII	October 10	October 24	Tokyo	Japan
1968	XIX	October 12	October 27	Mexico City	Mexico
1972	XX	August 26	September 11	Munich	Germany
1976	XXI	July 17	August 1	Montreal	Canada
1980	XXII	July 19	August 3	Moscow	Soviet Union (USSR)
1984	XXIII	July 28	August 12	Los Angeles, CA	United States
1988	XXIV	September 17	October 2	Seoul	South Korea
1992	XXV	July 25	August 9	Barcelona	Spain
1996	XXVI	July 19	August 4	Atlanta, GA	United States
2000	XXVII	September 15	October 1	Sydney	Australia
2004	XXVIII	August 13	August 29	Athens	Greece
2008	XXIX	August 8	August 24	Beijing	China
2012	XXX	July 27	August 12	London	England
2016	XXXI	August 5	August 21	Rio de Janeiro	Brazil

The Fourth Time's the Charm *(cont.)*

Name: _____

Part 1: Read each idea. Which source gives you this information? Fill in the correct bubble for each source. (Note: More than one bubble may be filled in for each idea.)

Information	Sources ➡	1	2	3	4
1. Olympiads are numbered using Roman numerals.		○	○	○	○
2. The Games of the I Olympiad took place in 1896.		○	○	○	○
3. The Games of the I Olympiad took place in Athens, Greece.		○	○	○	○
4. The London Games in 2012 took place during the XXX Olympiad.		○	○	○	○

Part 2: Fill in the bubble(s) next to the best answer(s) to each question.

5. During which Olympiad was there the longest span of time between the Opening Ceremonies and the Closing Ceremonies?

Ⓐ II Olympiad

Ⓑ III Olympiad

Ⓒ IV Olympiad

Ⓓ VI Olympiad

6. Which geographical facts can you infer by putting information together from Sources 1 and 4?

Ⓐ Australia is located in the Southern Hemisphere

Ⓑ South America and Australia are near one another.

Ⓒ Mexico City is located in the Northern Hemisphere.

Ⓓ Brazil is located in the country of Mexico.

7. The XXXIV Olympiad is due to take place in the year 2028. What number is represented by the Roman numeral XXXIV?

Ⓐ 34   Ⓑ 35   Ⓒ 36   Ⓓ 44

8. What was the last day of the XX Olympiad?

Ⓐ December 31, 1935

Ⓑ December 31, 1972

Ⓒ December 31, 1975

Ⓓ December 31, 1976

Part 3: Search "The Fourth Time's the Charm" to find **four-syllable words** with the following definitions. Then write the number of the source in which you located this information.

9. "without a doubt" _____   Source #: _____

10. "fit in with the needs of" _____   Source #: _____

The Fourth Time's the Charm *(cont.)*

Name: _____

Part 4: Refer back to the sources, and use complete sentences to answer questions #12 and #13.

11. Look at the pie chart below. Each portion represents host cities according to the number of times they have hosted the Olympic Games.

A. Which cities would belong in the "Twice" section?

_____

_____

B. Which city would belong in "Three Times" section?

_____

12. As a result of World War II, in which Olympiads were no Olympic Games held? Give your answer and explain how you came up with it.

_____

_____

_____

_____

_____

13. The title of this unit ("The Fourth Time's the Charm") is a play on a common saying mentioned elsewhere in the sources.

A. What is the common saying?

_____

B. What does this common saying mean?

_____

_____

C. How does "the fourth time's the charm" relate to the host city of the Games of the XXXI Olympiad?

_____

_____

_____

_____

February 29, 2100

Read each source below. Then complete the activities on pages 37–38.

Source 1

My little brother Zeet was born on February 29, 2092. Mom always tells Zeet that he's a special boy who has a special birthday. After all, February 29th doesn't come along every year. As far as I can tell, it comes along every four!

For the first few years of Zeet's life, he wasn't really aware of birthdays, so it didn't matter that we celebrated his on February 28th or March 1st. Then, when Zeet turned 4 on February 29, 2096, we had a big celebration. Even though that day was a Wednesday, our whole family took the day off of work and school to enjoy a warm, summer day at the beach.

Today is February 1, 2100, and it is Zeet's turn to change the screen on the digital calendar in our kitchen. He is very excited to see on what day his "real" birthday will fall this year. "I've been waiting four long years!" says Zeet.

"That's half your life," I say.

Zeet pushes an arrow key, and the display flips from January to February. With his finger, he traces down the screen until he gets to the end of the month. His finger stops on the blank square after the 28th. "Where is it?" asks Zeet. "There's no 29th! Mom, this calendar is defective!"

Source 2

Excerpt from *Tracking Time*

In 46 BCE, the Roman leader Julius Caesar introduced a new solar calendar. It was based on the fact that it takes Earth slightly more than 365 days to revolve around the Sun. This new calendar, named the Julian calendar, inserted an extra day exactly once every four years. This day is called a leap day, and the year in which it is inserted is called a leap year. Adding an extra day every four years meant that the average year on a Julian calendar is exactly 365.25 days long. This proved to be a bit too long.

As a result, a change was made in 1582 CE. A new calendar—called the Gregorian calendar—altered the number of leap days. This helped the new calendar conform more exactly to the solar year.

Under the new rules:

▶ Every year that is exactly divisible by 4 is a leap year, *except*

▶ Years that are exactly divisible by 100 are not leap years, *unless*

▶ A year is exactly divisible by 400, then it is a leap year.

This means that an average year on the Gregorian calendar is exactly 365.2425 days long.

Source 3

Listed here are the months in which the seasons begin in each hemisphere.

Hemisphere	Spring	Summer	Fall	Winter
Northern	March	June	September	December
Southern	September	December	March	June

Name: _____

Part 1: Look at each year listed. Determine if it is a leap year or not. Complete each column in the chart by writing **Yes** or **No**. Use the rules in Source 2 to help you.

	Year	Divisible by 4?	Divisible by 100?	Divisible by 400?	Leap Year?
1.	2000				
2.	2200				
3.	3000				
4.	4444				

Part 2: Fill in the bubble next to the best answer to each question.

5. In Source 1, Zeet thinks the calendar is defective. Which of these things could best be described as defective?

Ⓐ A light bulb that is turned off.

Ⓑ An old pen that has run out of ink.

Ⓒ A new tire that keeps going flat.

Ⓓ New shoes that don't fit very well.

6. When will Zeet be able to next celebrate his birthday on a February 29th?

Ⓐ 2100

Ⓑ 2102

Ⓒ 2104

Ⓓ 2112

7. From the information given, what can you infer about Zeet's family?

Ⓐ They use a Gregorian calendar.

Ⓑ They use a Julian calendar.

Ⓒ They have read *Tracking Time*.

Ⓓ They live in a large house.

8. From the information given, what can we infer about the narrator of Source 1?

Ⓐ He is older than 8 years old.

Ⓑ He did not go to school on February 29, 2096.

Ⓒ His birthday is not February 29, 2096.

Ⓓ all of the above

Ⓔ none of the above

Part 3: Search "February 29, 2100" to find one example of each of the following. Then write the number of the source in which you located this information.

9. smallest number that contains a decimal point _____   Source #: _____

10. word meaning "capable of being divided" _____   Source #: _____

Name: _____

Part 4: Refer back to the sources, and use complete sentences to answer these questions.

11. What is the setting (time and place) of Source 1? Circle the correct one below, and then explain how you know this is the answer. In your answer, use a quote from Source 1.

| in the present, in the Southern Hemisphere | in the future, in the Northern Hemisphere | in the future, in the Southern Hemisphere |

_____

_____

_____

_____

_____

12. Was the calendar in Zeet's home working properly? Why or why not? Why wouldn't there be a February 29, 2100? Provide evidence from another source to explain your answer.

_____

_____

_____

_____

_____

13. In Source 1, it is written that February 29, 2096, "was a Wednesday." Use the Internet to determine if this can be true. Enter "calendar 2096" into a search engine.

Will February 29, 2096, be a Wednesday? (Circle your answer.)   **Yes   No**

Now write your birthday in each row of the chart. Use an online calendar to find the day of the week on which your birthday will fall in the given years.

Your Birthday	Year	Day of the Week
	2032	
	2044	
	2076	

Baking Badly

Read each source below. Then complete the activities on pages 40–41.

Source 1

mise en place (pronounced *MEEZ en plas*) — French for "put in place"; in cooking, this term refers to the organizing and arranging of ingredients and equipment prior to cooking

---

Source 2

Aunt Edna's Brownies

Ingredients

1 cup sugar $\frac{1}{4}$ tsp. salt

$\frac{1}{3}$ cup melted butter $\frac{3}{4}$ cup flour

2 large eggs $\frac{1}{4}$ cup cocoa powder

Instructions

1. Preheat oven to 350°F.

2. In a large bowl, stir together the first three ingredients until well combined.

3. Add salt, flour, and cocoa powder to the egg mixture. Stir lightly.

4. Pour batter into a lightly greased 8" × 8" pan. Use a rubber spatula to smooth the mixture.

5. Bake for 20–25 minutes. Let cool before slicing.

Source 3

Dear Diary,

Things did not exactly go as planned today. I made Aunt Edna's famous brownies for Lisa's party, and they were really bad! In fact, I'm certain they could officially be called inedible. How did that happen? I read the recipe carefully. I even made an effort to be organized. I got my *mise en place* ready before I started cooking—just like they do on the fancy cooking shows Mom and I watch on TV. But clearly, something was very wrong with these brownies. I took one bite and had to spit it out. It tasted like a sweaty gym sock dipped in chocolate. It was the worst thing anyone has ever eaten. I'd better keep practicing if I'm ever going to be a contestant on *Kids in the Kitchen*.

Confused and embarrassed,
Dee

Source 4

Dee's *Mise en Place*

1 cup sugar

$\frac{1}{3}$ cup melted butter

2 large eggs

$\frac{1}{4}$ cup salt

$\frac{3}{4}$ cup flour

$\frac{1}{4}$ cup cocoa powder

bowl

pan

spatula

Baking Badly (cont.)

Name: _____

Part 1: Read each idea. Which source gives you this information? Fill in the correct bubble for each source. (Note: More than one bubble may be filled in for each idea.)

Information	Sources ➡	1	2	3	4
1. The pronunciation of a French cooking term.		○	○	○	○
2. The ingredients needed to make brownies.		○	○	○	○
3. Instructions for making brownies.		○	○	○	○
4. The name of the person whose recipe Dee made.		○	○	○	○

Part 2: Fill in the bubble next to the best answer to each question.

5. Which source shows an example of *mise en place*?

   Ⓐ Source 1   Ⓒ Source 3

   Ⓑ Source 2   Ⓓ Source 4

6. According to the recipe in Source 2, which ingredient would you use the least of to make Aunt Edna's brownies?

   Ⓐ salt   Ⓒ sugar

   Ⓑ flour   Ⓓ cocoa powder

7. To what does Dee compare the taste of her brownies?

   Ⓐ spoiled food   Ⓒ burnt rubber

   Ⓑ dirty clothing   Ⓓ sour milk

8. In Source 3, why is *Kids in the Kitchen* written in italic (slanted) type?

   Ⓐ It is the name of a cookbook.   Ⓒ It is the name of Dee's party.

   Ⓑ It is the name of a TV show.   Ⓓ It is from another language.

Part 3: Search "Baking Badly" to find one example of each of the following. Then write the number of the source in which you located this information.

9. word meaning "not suitable for eating" _____ Source #: _____

10. word meaning "one who takes part in a competition" _____ Source #: _____

Baking Badly (cont.)

Name: _____

Part 4: Refer back to the sources, and use complete sentences to answer these questions.

11. A writer or speaker uses *hyperbole* if he or she exaggerates greatly. In Source 3, find a quote that shows Dee using hyperbole. Write the exact quote, and then explain why it is an example of hyperbole.

Quote: _____

_____

Why?: _____

_____

_____

12. What did Dee do wrong? Why did her brownies taste awful? Use the information provided in the sources to explain your answer.

_____

_____

_____

_____

13. Name a food you like to eat for breakfast. Write it on the line. Your breakfast food can be as simple as cereal or as complicated as a fancy omelet. In the space below, draw your *mise en place* for your breakfast food. (Hint: Don't forget to include the equipment needed to make and eat the food.)

Name of Food: _____

Your *Mise en Place*:

The Winning Whiskers

Read each source below and on page 43. Then complete the activities on pages 44–45.

Source 1

This letter was mailed on October 15, 1860, from Westfield, New York, to Springfield, Illinois.

Hon A B Lincoln

Dear Sir

My father has just home from the fair and brought home your picture and Mr. Hamlin's. I am a little girl only eleven years old, but want you should be President of the United States very much so I hope you wont think me very bold to write to such a great man as you are. Have you any little girls about as large as I am if so give them my love and tell her to write to me if you cannot answer this letter. I have yet got four brothers and part of them will vote for you any way and if you let your whiskers grow I will try and get the rest of them to vote for you you would look a great deal better for your face is so thin. All the ladies like whiskers and they would tease their husbands to vote for you and then you would be President. My father is going to vote for you and if I was a man I would vote for you to but I will try to get every one to vote for you that I can I think that rail fence around your picture makes it look very pretty I have got a little baby sister she is nine weeks old and is just as cunning as can be. When you direct your letter direct to Grace Bedell Westfield Chautauqua County New York.

I must not write any more answer this letter right off Good bye

Grace Bedell

Source 2

The following letter was mailed on October 19, 1860, from Springfield, Illinois, to Westfield, New York.

Springfield, Ill Oct 19, 1860

Miss Grace Bedell

My dear little Miss

Your very agreeable letter of the 15th is received—I regret the necessity of saying I have no daughters—I have three sons—one seventeen, one nine, and one seven years of age. They, with their mother, constitute my whole family. As to the whiskers have never worn any, do you not think people would call it a silly affection if I were to begin it now?

Your very sincere well wisher

A. Lincoln

The Winning Whiskers *(cont.)*

Source 3

photograph of Abraham Lincoln
taken August 13, 1860

photograph of Abraham Lincoln
taken November 25, 1860

photograph of Abraham Lincoln
taken February 9, 1861

Source 4

Official Results
Presidential Election of 1860

held on Tuesday, November 6, 1860

Presidential Candidate	Popular Vote		Electoral Vote	
	Votes	Percentage	Votes	Percentage
Abraham Lincoln	1,855,993	39.65%	180	59.4%
John Breckinridge	851,844	18.20%	72	23.8%
John Bell	590,946	12.62%	39	12.9%
Stephen Douglas	1,381,944	29.52%	12	4.0%

The Winning Whiskers (cont.)

Name: _____

Part 1: Read each idea. Which source gives you this information? Fill in the correct bubble for each source. (Note: More than one bubble may be filled in for each idea.)

Information	Sources ➡	1	2	3	4
1. As of 1860, Lincoln had three sons.		○	○	○	○
2. Bell came in third in 1860's electoral vote.		○	○	○	○
3. Lincoln did not have a beard in August of 1860.		○	○	○	○
4. Lincoln began growing a beard in late 1860.		○	○	○	○

Part 2: Fill in the bubble next to the best answer to each question.

5. How many siblings does Grace mention in her letter to Lincoln?

Ⓐ 1

Ⓑ 2

Ⓒ 4

Ⓓ 5

6. About how long before the election did Grace send her letter to Lincoln?

Ⓐ three weeks

Ⓑ three months

Ⓒ six weeks

Ⓓ six months

7. Which of these most accurately describes Lincoln's response to Grace's urging that he grow "whiskers"?

Ⓐ It's true that I would look better with a beard.

Ⓑ I would look silly with a beard.

Ⓒ It might be too close to the election to change my look.

Ⓓ I want to earn your vote, so I will grow a beard.

8. Grace Bedell was born on November 4, 1848, and she died on November 2, 1936. How old was she on the day Abraham Lincoln was elected president of the United States?

Ⓐ 11

Ⓑ 12

Ⓒ 87

Ⓓ 88

Part 3: Search "The Winning Whiskers" to find one example of each of the following. Then write the number of the source in which you located this information.

9. number over one million _____ Source #: _____

10. greeting from a letter _____ Source #: _____

Part 4: Refer back to the sources, and use complete sentences to answer these questions.

11. Only men voted for president in the 1860 election. Until 1919, it was against the law for women to vote. Provide an exact 10-word quote that shows Grace Bedell was aware of this law.

_____

_____

12. Look at the pie charts below. They are created from the data given in Source 4. One shows the **popular vote** for the 1860 presidential election, while the other shows the **electoral vote**. Label each one correctly. Then explain the thought process you used in order to arrive at your answer.

A. _____   **B.** _____

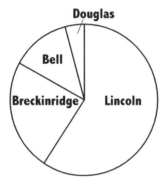

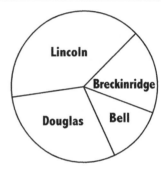

_____

_____

_____

_____

13. Did Abraham Lincoln's whiskers—his beard—help him win the election as Grace Bedell said it would? Give your answer—**Yes, No,** or **Not Enough Information to Answer**—and then explain why you feel this way.

_____

_____

_____

_____

_____

_____

Friggatriskaidekaphobia!*

Read each source below. Then complete the activities on pages 47–48.

You're Invited!

Our little Eve is officially becoming a teenager!

Date: *Friday, March 13, 2026*

Time: *7:00*

Place: *Eve's house*

RSVP: *to Eve by March 10ᵗʰ*
Phone: 552-2052
E-mail: eve31313@evemail.com

One More Thing:
It's Eve's golden birthday, so please wear gold for her special day!

Friday

1. the day between Thursday and Saturday

2. the last day of the workweek and first day of the weekend

3. the day named after Frigg, a Norse goddess

What a disaster! My birthday was on Friday, and for the occasion, my parents had planned an extravagant party at our house. Mom bought me a beautiful gold dress to wear. We sent out shiny, golden invitations. Mom and Sis hung gold streamers and other decorations around our house. And then Friday came, and no one showed up.

First, Aunt Ana and Uncle Bob RSVP'd with a "no." Then Cousin Otto said he couldn't come. Next, it was Grandma Hannah who wrote, "I'm so sorry, Eve. I'll stop by on Saturday to see you." The worst was when my best friend, Elle, said her parents wouldn't let her go. She begged and pleaded, but they offered up some weak excuse like, "not on that day."

When I told Dad that, he figured it out. He said that all those people must be afraid to leave their houses on a Friday the 13ᵗʰ. He said some people have a phobia about that day. "Really?" I thought, "How silly!" I know that a phobia is an irrational fear, but I just don't understand it. The number "13" has always been one of my favorites, but maybe that's because of the year I was born in. As for Friday, isn't it just another day of the week?

Glossary

golden birthday — when a person turns the age of his or her birth day (for example, when a person turns 10 years old on the 10ᵗʰ day of a month)

palindrome — a word, number, or phrase that reads the same backward as forward

* This word is pronounced *fri-guh-tris-kī-deck-uh-foe-bee-uh.*

Friggatriskaidekaphobia! *(cont.)*

Name: _____

Part 1: Read each idea. Which source gives you this information? Fill in the correct bubble for each source. (Note: More than one bubble may be filled in for each idea.)

Information	Sources ➡	1	2	3	4
1. *Friday* is named after a Norse goddess.		◯	◯	◯	◯
2. Eve has a cousin named Otto.		◯	◯	◯	◯
3. There is such a thing as a golden birthday.		◯	◯	◯	◯
4. The birthday party is at Eve's house.		◯	◯	◯	◯

Part 2: Fill in the bubble next to the best answer to each question.

5. How many syllables are in the word *friggatriskaidekaphobia*?

Ⓐ 7 Ⓒ 9

Ⓑ 8 Ⓓ 10

6. What do all of the people's names in Source 3 have in common?

Ⓐ They are all palindromes. Ⓒ They all begin with a vowel.

Ⓑ They all contain one syllable. Ⓓ They all name members of Eve's family.

7. What is the main purpose of the asterisk at the end of the title "Friggatriskaidekaphobia!"?

Ⓐ to show strong emotion

Ⓑ to show that more information is to follow

Ⓒ to show that this word will be defined below

Ⓓ to show that it is the longest word in the English language

8. Many of the people in Eve's life seem to suffer from friggatriskaidekaphobia. What would be the most accurate definition of this word?

Ⓐ a dislike of the number 13 Ⓒ an irrational fear of the number 13

Ⓑ a dislike of Friday the 13th Ⓓ an irrational fear of Friday the 13th

Part 3: Search "Friggatriskaidekaphobia!" to find one example of each of the following. Then write the number of the source in which you located this information.

9. number that is a palindrome _____ Source #: _____

10. abbreviation used as a verb _____ Source #: _____

Name: _____

Part 4: Refer back to the sources, and use complete sentences to answer these questions.

11. On what date was Eve born? Write it here: _____

On the lines below, cite as much evidence as you can to show how you came to this conclusion.

_____

_____

_____

_____

_____

_____

12. Using what you know about the number of days in a month, what is the oldest possible age at which a person could have their golden birthday? Explain how you arrived at this answer.

_____

_____

_____

_____

_____

_____

13. Have you already had your golden birthday? Circle one: **Yes**   **No**

- If so, how old were you, and what was the exact date on which it happened?

_____

_____

- If not, how old will you be, and what is the exact date on which it will happen?

_____

_____

Everything Floats

Read each source below. Then complete the activities on pages 50–51.

Source 1

Nina dipped her toes into the warm water. Though she had lived just 50 kilometers from the Dead Sea her whole life, this would be her first time "swimming" in it. In fact, Nina had never swum in any large body of water. She was horribly afraid of sharks, but her cousin had assured her that no sharks lived in the Dead Sea. He said, "There aren't any fish or even plants in there. Only microscopic animals like fungi can survive in that environment." Her cousin then gave Nina three tips for enjoying herself:

1. Don't splash the water,

2. Don't try to swim, and

3. Keep the water out of your mouth and especially your eyes.

He said the trick was to submerge yourself up to your waist and then gently lie back.

Nina did this, and up came her feet! They popped right to the surface. Nina looked around. All of the other "swimmers" were lying back and lounging on the water's surface. None of them were wearing life vests or using rafts. Nina had heard that you couldn't sink in the Dead Sea even if you tried!

After floating for ten minutes, Nina emerged from the water and lay on a lounge chair by the shore. In minutes, the blazing sun had dried her skin. It was then that she noticed that her legs and shoulders were caked with a white, grainy substance.

Source 2

Bodies of Water

Name	Region	Percentage of Salt Content
Dead Sea	Middle East	34.2%
Great Salt Lake	United States	5–27%
Atlantic Ocean	*many*	3.5%
Pacific Ocean	*many*	3.0%

Source 3

Jim said to his little brother, "Want to see a magic trick? Want to see me make an egg float in this glass of water?"

Nick nodded, so Jim dropped his egg into a red plastic cup that had already been filled with water. He waved his hand over the water, and said, "Rise!" The egg rose to the top of the cup and floated there.

Nick shook his head. "I can do that, too. Give me a cup."

Nick grabbed a blue plastic cup, filled it with water, and dropped his egg in. It sunk to the bottom and stayed there. "No fair," said Nick. "You used a red cup. I bet that's your trick!"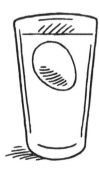

Everything Floats (cont.)

Name: _____

Part 1: Read each idea. Which source gives you this information? Fill in the correct bubble for each source. (Note: More than one bubble may be filled in for each idea.)

Information	Sources ➡	1	2	3
1. The Atlantic is saltier than the Pacific.		○	○	○
2. The Dead Sea is in the Middle East.		○	○	○
3. Fish don't live in the Dead Sea.		○	○	○
4. Fungi can live in the Dead Sea.		○	○	○

Part 2: Fill in the bubble next to the best answer to each question.

5. Which is not one of Nina's cousin's tips for being in the Dead Sea?

Ⓐ Don't splash in it.　　　　　　Ⓒ Don't drink it.

Ⓑ Don't swim in it.　　　　　　　Ⓓ Don't use a life vest in it.

6. What caused the egg in Jim's cup to float?

Ⓐ the wave of his hand　　　　　Ⓒ the words he spoke

Ⓑ the color of his cup　　　　　　Ⓓ something we didn't see him do

7. Which of these bodies of water has the greatest **range** of salinity (salt content)?

Ⓐ Dead Sea　　　　　　　　　　Ⓒ Atlantic Ocean

Ⓑ Great Salt Lake　　　　　　　　Ⓓ Pacific Ocean

8. In Source 1, why are the words "swimming" and "swimmers" written in quotation marks?

Ⓐ Nina said these words aloud to her cousin.

Ⓑ Her cousin said these words aloud to Nina.

Ⓒ The words don't give a true picture of what the people are doing.

Ⓓ Nina's cousin told her not to call the people "swimmers."

Part 3: Search "Everything Floats" to find one example each of words with the following meanings. Then write the number of the source in which you located this information.

9. "lying in a relaxed way" _____　Source #: _____

10. "too small to see with the naked eye" _____　Source #: _____

Everything Floats (cont.)

Name: _____

Part 4: Refer back to the sources, and use complete sentences to answer these questions.

11. The Dead Sea has had many names, including "the Sea of Salt" and "the Eastern Sea." Why do you think it is often called the Dead Sea? Cite evidence in your answer.

_____

_____

_____

_____

_____

_____

12. The circle below has been divided into 20 sections. This circle represents the water in the Dead Sea. First, answer this question: what percentage of water does each section represent? Write your answer in this box:

Now shade in the correct number of sections to show the percentage of salt in the Dead Sea. (Hint: Begin by rounding the percentage up to the nearest whole number.)

13. What might Jim have done to make his egg float? Why didn't the egg float in Nick's cup? Use what you have learned from the other sources to give evidence for your answer.

_____

_____

_____

_____

_____

_____

Just Deserts

Read each source below and on page 53. Then complete the activities on pages 54–55.

Source 1

"just deserts"

idiom meaning "a reward or punishment that is considered to be what the person getting it deserves"

(**Note:** This idiom is often misspoken or miswritten as "just desserts." One meaning of the word *desert* that is no longer used comes from the Latin language and means "deserve.")

Source 2

"Ready for the big hike?" Todd inquired of Sam.

Sam nodded. "In fact, I'm just returning from the store. I bought a lot of special gear for our trek."

Todd smiled, "Here's all the equipment I need: a pair of tennis shoes, one bottle of water, and my own two feet."

"I like to be extra prepared, I guess," said Sam. "I bought goggles to cover my eyes and a scarf to cover my nose, ears, and mouth. I bought a special canteen for holding lots of water. I also bought this lightweight jacket made of a special heat-saving material. That's just in case we're still out there when the sun goes down."

Todd laughed, "A jacket? In the desert? Where did you get a crazy idea like that?"

"From camels," said Sam. "I thought about camels and how they are perfectly adapted to life in the desert. Then I thought about how I could make myself more like a camel."

Source 3

What a nightmare. Let me go on record as saying that hiking in the desert is a bad idea. I don't know why I agreed to do it. First of all, it's hot—really hot. The sun beats down on you like an angry insect that you cannot swat away. Then the wind kicks up. I'm not talking about a gentle breeze. I'm talking about a whipping wind that spits skin-stinging sand at you from every direction. The sand gets in your eyes, your ears, your mouth—it even gets in your nose!

I trudged and stumbled through this harsh environment. The only two colors I saw for hours were the light brown of the sand and the blinding white of the sun. Then, mercifully, the sun began to lose strength and dip below the horizon. But this brought a whole new set of problems. Suddenly, the stifling heat of the day was replaced by the shiver-inducing cold of the night. As I staggered back to our car at the end of a long day, I reminded myself to do exactly what Sam does next time. She always does her research and knows what she is getting herself into. The whole time, she traipsed along with a big smile on her face. At the end, she even looked warm and comfy in her special jacket. Who would think to bring a jacket into the desert?

Source 4

Mr. Blake said, "Camels live in deserts, and they are perfectly suited for that type of environment. Let's look at this diagram I have drawn up on the board. It illustrates some of the difficulties associated with desert living, and it explains the natural defenses camels have to combat these difficulties."

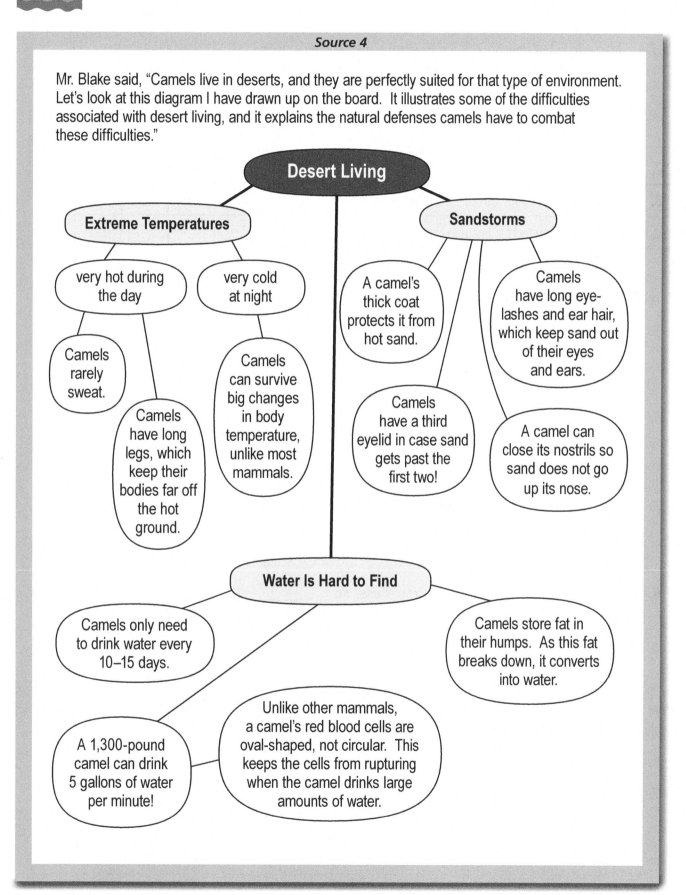

Just Deserts *(cont.)*

Name: _____

Part 1: Read each idea from Source 3. In which paragraph in Source 3 is this information located? Fill in the correct bubble. (Note: More than one bubble may be filled in for each idea.)

Information	Paragraphs ➡	1	2	3	4
1. A person named Sam is going on a desert walk.		○	○	○	○
2. A person named Todd is going on a desert walk.		○	○	○	○
3. Sam is well prepared for the desert walk.		○	○	○	○
4. Camels are well suited for living in deserts.		○	○	○	○

Part 2: Fill in the bubble next to the best answer to each question.

5. Which of these hyphenated words from the sources means "very cold"?

Ⓐ heat-saving

Ⓑ skin-stinging

Ⓒ shiver-inducing

Ⓓ oval-shaped

6. Which of the sources is written in the first-person voice?

Ⓐ Source 1

Ⓑ Source 2

Ⓒ Source 3

Ⓓ Source 4

7. Which of these words conveys a different meaning than the others?

Ⓐ trudged

Ⓑ traipsed

Ⓒ staggered

Ⓓ stumbled

8. Sam brings a scarf to use in the way a camel uses its _____.

Ⓐ nostrils

Ⓑ third eyelid

Ⓒ long eyelashes

Ⓓ hump

Part 3: Search "Just Deserts" to find words with the following meanings. Then write the number of the source in which you located this information.

9. "changes" or "transforms" _____ Source #: _____

10. "sweets eaten after meals" _____ Source #: _____

Just Deserts *(cont.)*

Name: _____

Part 4: Refer back to the sources, and use complete sentences to answer these questions.

11. Does the idiom from Source 1 apply to Sam or Todd (or does it apply to both)? Use evidence from the sources to defend your answer.

_____

_____

_____

_____

_____

12. The author of Source 3 uses a simile to compare one thing to another thing. Locate this simile and quote the entire sentence in the box below.

13. Look at the picture of the camel. Explain which body parts are especially adapted to desert living. The first one is done for you. Label four more.

A camel's long legs keep its body away from the hot ground.

The Unneeded Earmuffs

Read each source below. Then complete the activities on pages 57–58.

Source 1

Juan was panicked. "This is going to cost me an arm and a leg! The airline charges for each suitcase you bring on an international flight. Help!"

Amy looked at what Juan had packed. "Sweaters, scarves, a ski jacket? Earmuffs? Where are you going, Antarctica?"

"Very funny. Listen, I just spoke with Maria. She said the temperatures in Alicante have been nearly 35°, and she expects it to *cool off soon*. How much more can it cool off? It's already almost freezing!"

"Wow, Spain gets that cold in August?"

"My Spanish isn't so hot, but I think Maria said the temperatures have been extreme lately. This is terrible timing. I was looking forward to relaxing on the beach and swimming in the sea."

"Good luck with that!" said Amy.

Source 3

Mr. Shirk pointed at the large thermometer projected onto the class's whiteboard.

"Here we have the two major scales by which we measure temperature. You might notice that the numbers on the left side have an *F* above them. That's because they show the Fahrenheit scale. That's the one we use here in the United States. On this scale, water boils at 212° and freezes at 32°. This scale is also used in a handful of small countries, such as Belize, Bermuda, and Jamaica. Now the rest of the world, along with the *entire* scientific community, recognizes a different scale. They use Celsius (C). On this scale, water boils at 100° and freezes at 0°. Now isn't that easier to remember?"

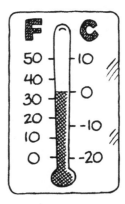

Source 2

Formula to convert Celsius (C) temperatures to Fahrenheit (F)

Step	Action
❶	Multiply the Celsius temperature by 9.
❷	Then divide by 5.
❸	Then add 32 to the result.

Source 4

Average daily temperatures for summer months in Alicante, Spain (both in Celsius and Fahrenheit)

	June	July	August
Average High °C (°F)	27.2 (81)	30.1 (86.2)	30.6 (87.1)
Average Low °C (°F)	17.1 (62.8)	19.7 (67.5)	20.4 (68.7)

The Unneeded Earmuffs *(cont.)*

Name: _____

Part 1: Read each idea. Which source gives you this information? Fill in the correct bubble for each source. (Note: More than one bubble may be filled in for each idea.)

Information	Sources ➡	1	2	3	4
1. "C" is the abbreviation for "Celsius."		○	○	○	○
2. Water boils at 212°F.		○	○	○	○
3. Alicante is in Spain.		○	○	○	○
4. Scientists use the Celsius scale.		○	○	○	○

Part 2: Fill in the bubble next to the best answer to each question.

5. What exactly does Juan mean when he says his "Spanish isn't so hot"?

Ⓐ Spanish is not a warm language.

Ⓑ He does not speak Spanish well.

Ⓒ He does not understand Spanish well.

Ⓓ He sounds cold when he speaks Spanish.

6. Which of these is the warmest temperature?

Ⓐ 0°C

Ⓑ 0°F

Ⓒ 3°C

Ⓓ 30°F

7. Which of the following is an accurate way to express the formula for converting Celsius temperatures to the Fahrenheit scale?

Ⓐ $(C \times 9) + 5 \div 32 = F$

Ⓑ $(C \times 9) \div 5 + 32 = F$

Ⓒ $C \times (9 \div 5) + 32 = F$

Ⓓ $C \times 9 \div (5 + 32) = F$

8. Which of these is **not** information we can infer from Source 1?

Ⓐ Juan and Amy are brother and sister.

Ⓑ Juan has packed more than one suitcase.

Ⓒ Amy is not going to Spain with Juan.

Ⓓ Antarctica is a cold place.

Part 3: Search "The Unneeded Earmuffs" to find one example of each of the following. Then write the number of the source in which you located this information.

9. name for a device that measures temperature _____   Source #: _____

10. word meaning "between two or more countries" _____   Source #: _____

Name: _____

Part 4: Refer back to the sources, and use complete sentences to answer these questions.

11. Mr. Shirk seems to favor one temperature scale over the other. Name the scale he prefers. Then provide quotes from the text that lead us to conclude that he favors one over the other.

_____

_____

_____

_____

12. Why are Juan's earmuffs unneeded (along with his other winter clothes)? Using the Fahrenheit scale and the formula in Source 3, calculate the temperature at Maria's home in Alicante. Use your results to explain what Maria meant when she said "the temperatures have been extreme lately."

_____

_____

_____

_____

_____

13. Repack Juan's suitcase for him. Using the average temperature in August in Alicante, make a list of clothing Juan should pack.

Things I'll Need in Spain

A Fallible Friend

Read each source below. Then complete the activities on pages 60–61.

Source 1

After handing out the homework assignment, Ms. Hart cautioned her class, "Now, please please PLEASE remember to read over your essays before turning them in. Make sure your punctuation is correct and you have not made any spelling errors. Do not simply use the spellcheck function on your computer and assume that will be adequate. Yes, spellcheck can be your friend, but it is not *infallible*. It is not perfect. It does not know everything. It makes mistakes."

She continued, "It's true that spellcheck will catch obvious spelling errors such as F-R-E-I-N-D or F-A-M-I-L-L-Y. A squiggly underline will appear under the word, and you will know that the word needs to be corrected. But spellcheck often misses more subtle mistakes. What if you spell a word correctly, but it's not the correct word for the sentence? Spellcheck won't, for example, catch a misused homophone. *There*, *their*, and *they're* may all sound the same to you, but they all *look* the same to spellcheck. No, nothing beats the human eyes and the human brain... so use yours! Your grade depends on it."

Source 2

A **prefix** is a word part that is placed in front of a base word and changes the base word's meaning in some way. In English, there are several prefixes that mean "not" and add a negative meaning to the base word. Here are a few such prefixes:

dis — *dishonest* means "not honest"

il — *illegal* means "not legal"

im — *immature* means "not mature"

in — *inexact* means "not exact"

ir — *irresponsible* means "not responsible"

un — *unlikely* means "not likely"

Source 3

My Favorite Hobby

by J.T. Willis

Fishing is fun fore many reasons. It is relaxxing to be in a boat on a lake or in a pond. These places ofer piece and quiet.

I also love catching dinner for my famille. Theirs nuthing better than fresh fish cooked over a fire.

I once cot a really wierd fish. Dad said we should throw it back in the water. That's what we did.

A Fallible Friend *(cont.)*

Name: _____

Part 1: Read each idea. Which source gives you this information? Fill in the correct bubble for each source. (Note: More than one bubble may be filled in for each idea.)

Information	Sources ➡	1	2	3
1. *Family* is not spelled f-a-m-i-l-l-y.		○	○	○
2. Several prefixes mean "not."		○	○	○
3. A prefix changes a base word's meaning.		○	○	○
4. *There*, *their*, and *there* are homophones.		○	○	○

Part 2: Fill in the bubble next to the best answer to each question.

5. Homophones are words that

Ⓐ sound the same.

Ⓑ have the same meanings.

Ⓒ have different meanings.

Ⓓ Both A and B.

Ⓔ Both A and C.

6. Which of the following errors might not be caught by spellcheck?

Ⓐ *its* instead of *it's*

Ⓑ *mits* instead of *mitts*

Ⓒ *boxs* instead of *boxes*

Ⓓ *wierd* instead of *weird*

7. You can infer that some words are underlined in Source 3 because

Ⓐ they are spelled incorrectly.

Ⓑ they are vocabulary words.

Ⓒ they show the main idea of the story.

Ⓓ they contain prefixes.

8. The phrase "not infallible" is an example of a

Ⓐ double prefix.

Ⓑ double negative.

Ⓒ double meaning.

Ⓓ spelling error.

Part 3: Search "A Fallible Friend" to find one example of each of the following. Then write the number of the source in which you located this information.

9. word meaning "used wrongly" _____ Source #: _____

10. word meaning "not precise" _____ Source #: _____

A Fallible Friend (cont.)

Name: _____

Part 4: Refer back to the sources, and use complete sentences to answer these questions.

11. Use the information and the context clues in Sources 1 and 2 to determine the meaning of *infallible* and *fallible*. Give the definitions for each, and then explain the process you used to determine the meanings of these words.

Infallible means _____

_____

_____

Fallible means _____

_____

_____

12. In Source 3, the author misused four homophones. Find the four homophones and write them below. Then correctly spell the word he should have used in each instance. The first misused homophone is written for you.

	Misused Homophone	**Correct Word**
❶	fore	
❷		
❸		
❹		

13. The "friend" mentioned in the title "A Fallible Friend" is not a person, it's a thing (spellcheck). Is there an object or thing that you rely on so much that you would call it a friend? If so, explain how your "friend" has helped you. If not, explain why you think this is so.

_____

_____

_____

_____

_____

_____

Pioneers in Space

Read each source below. Then complete the activities on pages 63–65.

Source 1

astronaut

1. from the Greek words *astron* meaning "star" and *nautes* meaning "sailor"

2. In English-speaking countries, an astronaut is a person who is trained to travel on or is traveling on a spacecraft.

3. In Russian/Soviet countries, such a person is referred to as a cosmonaut (from the Greek *kosmos* meaning "universe" and *nautes* meaning "sailor")

Source 2

Dear Sasha,

In class today, we learned about the history of Russian space travel. Wow, your country-men accomplished a lot of firsts in space travel. Of course, you live in Russia, but it was called the Soviet Union back then.

Mr. Roman taught us that a dog named Laika was the first animal to orbit Earth. The Soviet space program sent Laika into orbit way back in 1957. Poor Laika did not survive the flight.

In 1961, a man named Yuri Gagarin became the first human to orbit Earth. He flew on a ship called Vostok 1, and he did survive. Just two years later aboard Vostok 6, Valentina Tereshkova became the first woman in space. Two years after that, Alexei Leonov was the first person to walk in space. On March 18, 1965, he spent 10 minutes outside of his spaceship. I cannot imagine being the first person to ever do something like that. All of these Soviet astronauts must have been very brave!

Your friend,
Andrew

Source 3

If you remember, class, we talked yesterday about such space pioneers as John Glenn who, in 1962, became the first American to orbit Earth. In 1998, the 77-year-old Glenn also earned the distinction of being the oldest person to fly into space.

We also read about Neil Armstrong. During the *Apollo 11* mission, this legendary astronaut became the first person to walk on the moon. This happened on July 20, 1969.

Now please open your *America's Space Pioneers* textbooks to chapter 5, "Women in Space." Today, we will be reading about such American heroes as Sally Ride and Eileen Collins. In 1983, Ms. Ride became the first American woman in space. (I should point out here that a Soviet cosmonaut by the name of Valentina Tereshkova was the first woman in space, a feat she accomplished two decades earlier.) In 1995, Eileen Collins became the first female to pilot a U.S. mission in space.

Okay, let's have someone read the first paragraph. Do I have any volunteers?

Pioneers in Space *(cont.)*

Name: _____

Part 1: Read each idea. Which source gives you this information? Fill in the correct bubble for each source. (Note: More than one bubble may be filled in for each idea.)

Information	Sources ➡	1	2	3
1. The first animal in space did not survive.		○	○	○
2. Valentina Tereshkova was the first woman in space.		○	○	○
3. The word *astronaut* has Greek origins.		○	○	○
4. A human first orbited Earth in 1961.		○	○	○

Part 2: Fill in the bubble next to the best answer to each question.

5. Who was the first female to pilot a ship into space?

    Ⓐ Valentina Tereshkova   Ⓒ Sally Ride

    Ⓑ Alexei Leonov   Ⓓ Eileen Collins

6. If you combine the meaning of its Greek root words, what exactly does the word *astronaut* mean?

    Ⓐ "star sailor"   Ⓒ "space pioneer"

    Ⓑ "star traveler"   Ⓓ "space traveler"

7. In writing, *italic* (or slanted) type is used to distinguish certain types of words. Find all of the ways in which *italic type* is used in "Pioneers in Space." Which is not a way that it is used?

    Ⓐ for the names of spaceships   Ⓒ for the name of book titles

    Ⓑ for words in a foreign language   Ⓓ for the name of chapters in a book

8. From the information given in Source 2, the reader can infer that one of the following is a fact. Which one is a fact?

    Ⓐ Andrew is American.   Ⓒ Andrew is a high-school student.

    Ⓑ Andrew is not Russian.   Ⓓ Andrew is studying to be an astronaut.

Part 3: Search "Pioneers in Space" to find one example of each of the following. Then write the number of the source in which you located this information.

9. two-word phrase meaning "20 years" _____ Source #: _____

10. homophone for the plural of "foot" _____ Source #: _____

Pioneers in Space *(cont.)*

Name: _____

Part 4: Refer back to the sources, and use complete sentences to answer these questions.

11. Look back at Source 2. What mistake does Andrew make near the end of his letter? Pretend you are Sasha. Write a one- or two-line text message to Andrew, explaining the mistake he made. Use a friendly, helpful tone in your message.

12. Think back on the feats described in Sources 2 and 3. Which do you think would have been the most exciting to accomplish? Which would have been the most frightening? On the lines below, choose one feat on which to focus. Tell your feelings about it and why you think you would have been most excited or frightened to have done it.

_____

_____

_____

_____

_____

_____

_____

_____

_____

_____

_____

_____

Pioneers in Space *(cont.)*

Name: _____

Part 4 *(cont.)*:

13. Complete the timeline below. Some information has been filled in for you.

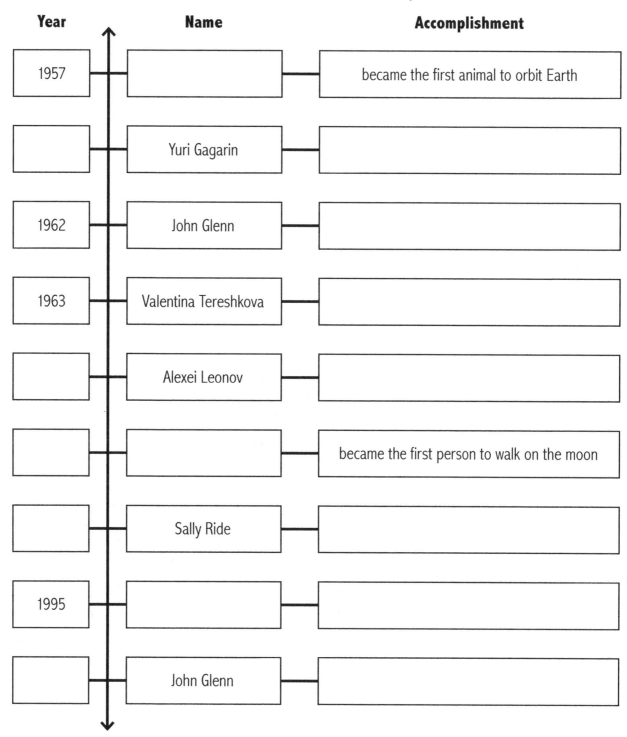

Year	Name	Accomplishment
1957		became the first animal to orbit Earth
	Yuri Gagarin	
1962	John Glenn	
1963	Valentina Tereshkova	
	Alexei Leonov	
		became the first person to walk on the moon
	Sally Ride	
1995		
	John Glenn	

A Grain of Salt

Read each source below. Then complete the activities on pages 67–68.

Source 1

idiom (noun) — a common saying whose figurative meaning is different from its literal meaning (example, "It's raining cats and dogs." There is a heavy rain, but animals are not actually raining from the sky.)

Source 2

Reviewer: Trish Thomas

Rating: ★★★★⯪

Grain of Salt is *the* new place in town, so my husband and I checked it out on Friday. The place was super busy! They could have used about two more cooks and three more waiters. It took a while to get our food, but it was well worth the wait. The corn chowder was silky smooth, and the halibut my husband ordered was incredibly fresh. Even our apple pie was yummy, and I don't usually like deserts. We will be coming back very soon.

Source 3

Reviewer: A. Foodie

Rating: ★★★★☆

Another reviewer hit the nail on the head: this eatery would be great if they hired more staff. The food was delicious, but it took FOREVER to get our meals. I could see the chef frantically cooking, and our server ran around like his pants were on fire. Nothing helped. We almost left, but I'm so glad we didn't. You have to try the shrimp nachos. They're heavenly!

Source 4

Reviewer: Vick Z.

Rating: ★★★★★

Whoa Grain of Salt They rockz! Saturday night with my buddys. Gourmet grub! Shrimp nachos! Avocaddo milkshakes! Monster TV in the lobby. Cyclones game on Touchdown! Im happy

---

Source 5

Reviewer: Todd Pepper

Rating: ★☆☆☆☆

It would take about a million more grains of salt to make this food edible. It was awful! I own the Pepper Mill down the street, so I dropped in one evening for a quick bite. That was my first mistake. At this place, "quick" means an hour wait. A professional restaurant should know how many waiters it needs to hire. But the real problem here is the bland, flavorless food. So if you want a fast, delicious dinner, head on over to the Pepper Mill. We'll treat you right!

A Grain of Salt *(cont.)*

Name: _____

Part 1: Read each idea. Which source gives you this information about the Grain of Salt restaurant? Fill in the correct bubble for each source. (Note: More than one bubble may be filled in for each idea.)

Information	Sources ➡	1	2	3	4	5
1. It has a TV in the lobby.		◯	◯	◯	◯	◯
2. It serves shrimp nachos.		◯	◯	◯	◯	◯
3. It needs more staff.		◯	◯	◯	◯	◯
4. It serves good food.		◯	◯	◯	◯	◯

Part 2: Fill in the bubble next to the best answer to each question.

5. Who gave the restaurant its highest rating?

    Ⓐ Trish Thomas   Ⓒ Vick Z.

    Ⓑ A. Foodie   Ⓓ Todd Pepper

6. Which of the reviewers ordered the halibut?

    Ⓐ Trish Thomas   Ⓒ Vick Z.

    Ⓑ A. Foodie   Ⓓ None of the above.

7. The reviewer in Source 2 made a spelling or usage error in her review. Which word is not spelled correctly in the way that it is used?

    Ⓐ busy   Ⓒ smooth

    Ⓑ waiters   Ⓓ deserts

8. Which of the following quotes from "A Grain of Salt" is an idiom?

    Ⓐ "Another reviewer hit the nail on the head"

    Ⓑ "Avocado milkshakes!"

    Ⓒ "That was my first mistake."

    Ⓓ "The place was super busy!"

Part 3: Search "A Grain of Salt" to find one example of a word that is emphasized in each of the following ways. Then write the number of the source in which you located this information.

9. through the use of italic (slanted) font _____ Source #: _____

10. through the use of all capital letters _____ Source #: _____

Name: _____

Part 4: Refer back to the sources, and use complete sentences to answer these questions.

11. Which reviewer made the most grammatical errors in his/her review? _____

In the space below, rewrite his/her review. Use complete sentences and correct grammar.

_____

_____

_____

_____

_____

12. "Take it with a grain of salt" is an idiom that means you should view something with skepticism. This means that you may not want to fully believe what you have heard or read. The writer or speaker may have reason to mislead you. Of the four reviewers, whose review should you probably "take with a grain of salt"?

_____

Cite evidence to support your answer.

_____

_____

_____

_____

_____

_____

13. A *pseudonym* is a made-up name, especially one used by an author. Which of the reviewers is most likely using a pseudonym?

_____

Now, it's your turn. Imagine you are a professional restaurant critic and that you want to use a pseudonym. Think of an appropriate pseudonym and write it here:

Winning Isn't Everything

Read each source below. Then complete the activities on pages 70–71.

Source 1

"Winning isn't everything; it's the only thing."

"Red" Sanders
college football coach

Source 2

"It's not that you won or lost but how you played the game."

Grantland Rice
sportswriter

Source 3

"The most important thing is not to win but to take part!"

Pierre de Courbertin
Olympic Games founder

Source 4

I was there on that September day in South Korea in 1988. I saw the whole thing. I had earned a spot in the Olympic Games, and I was racing my boat on a nearby course. The wind suddenly began to gust. By my instruments, the wind reached 35 knots. It was all I could do to control my boat and keep her from dumping me into the water. In the distance, I glimpsed a boat capsizing, and I saw two Olympic athletes thrown overboard. I knew they were injured and in real danger, but I could do nothing to help. That's when I saw Lawrence Lemieux spring to action. A Canadian sailor racing on a nearby course, Lemieux changed course and headed straight for the injured sailors. He saved their lives that day when he pulled them from the water. I was told later that he waited for a patrol vehicle to come rescue the sailors from his boat before he rejoined the race. I also heard that Lemieux was in second place when he veered off the course to help the sailors! Second place! And he ended up finishing the race in 22nd place. He sacrificed his chance for a gold or silver medal because he saw some people in need. To me, that is what the Olympic Games are all about.

I was so happy when I found out later that Lemieux was awarded the Pierre de Coubertin medal for sportsmanship. This was only the fifth time that award had been given. One could even say that it's more valuable and more special than an Olympic gold medal. I don't know what Lawrence Lemieux would say. Winning an Olympic medal was obviously not his first priority when he saw those two men fall into the stormy sea.

Source 5

Fiction is a type of writing that creates events or experiences. A **genre** is a category into which a piece of fictional literature belongs. Here are some examples of genres:

- **Fantasy** — creates an imaginary world filled with unnatural characters and events

- **Historical Fiction** — creates a fictional experience that involves a real person or event from the past

- **Mystery** — involves a crime that is committed and needs to be solved

- **Science Fiction** — creates a new world based on future scientific knowledge

Winning Isn't Everything *(cont.)*

Name: _____

Part 1: Read each idea. Which source gives you this information? Fill in the correct bubble for each source. (Note: More than one bubble may be filled in for each idea.)

Information Sources ➡	1	2	3	4	5
1. The 1988 Olympic Games were in South Korea.	○	○	○	○	○
2. A genre is a category of literature.	○	○	○	○	○
3. Grantland Rice was a sportswriter.	○	○	○	○	○
4. Lawrence Lemieux rescued two sailors.	○	○	○	○	○

Part 2: Fill in the bubble next to the best answer to each question.

5. The medal for sportsmanship that Lemieux was given is named after

Ⓐ a sportswriter.

Ⓑ an Olympic sailor.

Ⓒ a football coach.

Ⓓ the Olympic Games founder.

6. From the information given, you can infer that a wind of 40 knots is

Ⓐ gusting.

Ⓑ veering.

Ⓒ changing.

Ⓓ reaching.

7. Based on what he said or did, which person would most likely think that a gold medal is the most important thing you can get from the Olympic Games?

Ⓐ Lawrence Lemieux

Ⓑ "Red" Sanders

Ⓒ Grantland Rice

Ⓓ Pierre de Coubertin

8. Source 4 creates a character to narrate the story of Lawrence Lemieux's rescue of two injured sailors. Based on this, which of the genres listed in Source 5 best describes Source 4?

Ⓐ Fantasy

Ⓑ Historical Fiction

Ⓒ Mystery

Ⓓ Science Fiction

Part 3: Search "Winning Isn't Everything" to find one example of each of the following. Then write the number of the source in which you located this information.

9. word meaning "overturning in water" _____ Source #: _____

10. word meaning "gave up something of value" _____ Source #: _____

Winning Isn't Everything (cont.)

Name: _____

Part 4: Refer back to the sources, and use complete sentences to answer these questions.

11. Choose a quote from Source 1, 2, or 3. In the box, rewrite the quote exactly. Then, in your own words, explain what the quote means. Use an example from everyday life.

_____

_____

_____

_____

12. Think about what Lawrence Lemieux did. Which quote (Source 1, 2, or 3) best fits his actions during the 1988 Olympic Games? Explain your answer.

_____

_____

_____

_____

_____

_____

13. In Source 4, the narrator says that winning the Pierre de Coubertin medal for sportsmanship may be more valuable and special than winning an Olympic gold medal. Do you agree or disagree? Give reasons for your answer.

_____

_____

_____

_____

_____

_____

Two One-of-a-Kinds

Read each source below. Then complete the activities on pages 73–75.

Source 1

Phrase		What It Is		What It Means
"one of a kind"	➡	idiom	➡	the only item of a particular type

Source 2

That is a picture of me up there. I am a star-nosed mole, the most unique creature you will ever see.

I am a small mammal that lives in the northeastern part of North America. I can grow to about 8 inches in length; and I have a long tail, water-repellant fur, and 44 teeth. I eat mostly worms, insects, and crustaceans. Oh, and did I mention that I have an awesome nose?

My nose, or snout, is truly amazing, if I do say so myself. It is ringed by 11 pairs of pink, fleshy appendages. (Appendages are smaller parts that stick out of larger parts.) No other animal has a nose like this. And my snout is not just for looks! It is covered with about 25,000 tiny sensory receptors. Since I'm nearly blind, I need those receptors to gather information about my environment. Just how good is my star-shaped snout at doing this? Well, for starters, I am the only mammal that can smell underwater.

Having such a super special snout helps me to find food and gobble it up quickly. In fact, I am the world's fastest-eating mammal. Within 8 *milliseconds*, I can decide if a particle of food is worth eating or not. This is about as fast as a signal to the brain can travel. Within about 120 milliseconds, I can completely consume a meal. I guess you might say that I have a "fast food" diet.

For all these reasons and more, I would say that I am the most unique animal on the planet.

Source 3

A lot of animals like to think of themselves as unique, but really, is there any contest? I am a platypus, and I am certainly the most one-of-a-kind animal in the world. When I was first discovered in my native Australia, some experts even thought I was a joke being played on them. Let me explain.

I have the tail of a beaver and the fur of an otter. I have the bill and webbed feet of a duck. I am an expert swimmer, but when I leave the water, the webbing on my feet retracts. This exposes my bare knuckles, which I use to walk on. This is important, because I like to eat my food on land. You see, I gather up food in the water and store it in my cheek pouches. Then, when I get to land, I pick up pieces of gravel and use them to crush the food in my mouth. I do this because I don't have any teeth.

Having no teeth could make it difficult to defend myself, but luckily I have special spurs on my back feet that can be used to inject venom into my enemies. I am one of the few venomous mammals in the world. Along with a few anteaters, I am also one of the very few mammals that lays eggs.

For these and many other reasons, I believe I deserve to be called the most unique animal on Earth.

Two One-of-a-Kinds *(cont.)*

Name: _____

Part 1: Read each idea. Does it describe a star-nosed mole, a platypus, or neither? Fill in the correct bubble for each animal. (Note: More than one bubble may be filled in for each idea.)

Information Animal ➡	Star-nosed Mole	Platypus	Neither
1. This animal is a mammal.	○	○	○
2. This animal lays eggs.	○	○	○
3. This animal is not venomous.	○	○	○
4. This animal is native to South America.	○	○	○

Part 2: Fill in the bubble next to the best answer to each question.

5. Which of the following clues is **not** given as proof that platypuses spend a lot of time in the water?

Ⓐ They are expert swimmers. Ⓒ They can smell under water.

Ⓑ They have webbed feet. Ⓓ They gather their food in the water.

6. Which statement is true about a star-nosed mole? Complete the information in the box to help you.

Ⓐ It has more appendages on its nose than it has teeth.

Ⓑ It has $\frac{1}{2}$ as many appendages on its nose as it has teeth.

Ⓒ It has $\frac{1}{4}$ as many appendages on its nose as it has teeth.

Ⓓ It has twice as many appendages on its nose as it has teeth.

> Number of Teeth _____
>
> Number of Appendages _____

7. In both Source 2 and Source 3, what is the author's main purpose?

Ⓐ to persuade readers to accept an opinion

Ⓑ to give information about mammals

Ⓒ to entertain readers and show the personalities of different animals

Ⓓ to introduce readers to the animals of Australia

8. Both Source 2 and Source 3 end with what type of sentence?

Ⓐ introductory Ⓑ concluding Ⓒ interrogative Ⓓ exclamatory

Part 3: Search "Two One-of-a-Kinds" to find examples of verbs with the following meanings. Then write the number of the source in which you located this information.

9. "pulls back in" _____ Source #: _____

10. "eat" or "ingest" _____ Source #: _____

Name: _____

Part 4: Refer back to the sources, and use complete sentences to answer these questions.

11. Sources 2 and 3 are each written in the first-person voice. How would these sources be different if they were written in the third-person voice? How does the use of the first-person voice change the tone of the writing?

_____

_____

_____

_____

_____

12. Choose a side. Decide which of these two animals is the most "one-of-a-kind." Write a persuasive essay that makes your case. Use evidence gathered from Sources 2 and 3.

_____

_____

_____

_____

_____

_____

_____

_____

_____

_____

_____

_____

_____

_____

Part 4 (cont.):

13. Choose one of the categories below and circle it. Then write two persuasive essays from the perspective of two different animals. (Don't use the animals described in Sources 2 and 3.) In each essay, use the first-person voice to explain why this particular animal best represents the chosen category.

the smartest	the most dangerous	the most helpful	the strongest

Double the Fun!

Read each source below. Then complete the activities on pages 77–78.

A NEW MILLENNIUM?

January 1, 2000

As we say goodbye to the 1990s and hello to the 2000s, many people believe we are also welcoming in something else: the third millennium. A millennium* is a period of 1,000 years. So the question is, does the third millennium begin today or on January 1, 2001?

"Today is not the beginning of the third millennium," says historical scholar Earnest Grum. "There was never a year 0 on our calendar, and so the first millennium went from the year 1 to the year 1000. Thus, the second millennium should go from the year 1001 to 2000, and the third millennium does not begin until the first day of 2001."

A poll of people on the street reveals a different opinion. "This is the first day of the millennium," says carpenter Paul Folks. The decade of the '90s is over, the 20th century just ended, and so did the previous millennium. It's just common sense."

Many shared this view, and so the debate rages on. A consensus may never be reached, not even by the time the fourth millennium begins on January 1, 3000 (or January 1, 3001).

*As a side note, when asked to spell the word *millennium*, only 4 out of 24 people polled were able to do so correctly. The trick is to note that the word has two sets of double letters (two *l*s and two *n*s).

---

double letters

when the same vowel or consonant appears consecutively within a word (for example, *foot* or *ball*).

apple

moon

Nearly every morning, Otto Min awoke to the sounds of a raccoon scratching at the metallic roof of his house. Otto's morning routine was always the same: he made coffee, lifted a set of dumbbells twenty times, and was out the door by 6:00 sharp. Otto was a bookkeeper for the largest mattress manufacturer in Mississippi. On this very special morning for Otto, he was allowed access into a very important committee meeting. He wanted to make a good impression on his bosses. It occurred to him that he should enter the meeting with pizzazz and distinguish himself in some memorable way, but instead he hiccupped loudly when he shook his boss's hand. "How embarrassing!" he thought.

Double the Fun! *(cont.)*

Name: _____

Part 1: Read each idea. Which source gives you this information? Fill in the correct bubble for each source. (Note: More than one bubble may be filled in for each idea.)

Information	Sources ➡	1	2	3
1. The word *moon* contains a double letter.		○	○	○
2. A millennium is a period of 1,000 years.		○	○	○
3. *Millennium* has two sets of double letters.		○	○	○
4. *Football* has two sets of double letters.		○	○	○

Part 2: Fill in the bubble next to the best answer to each question.

5. What does the word *consecutively* mean as it is used in Source 2?

    Ⓐ occurring in an unbroken sequence   Ⓒ featuring double letters

    Ⓑ resulting from an action   Ⓓ happening as a consequence of

6. According to the fictional Earnest Grum (from Source 1), what will be the first day of the fourth millennium?

    Ⓐ January 1, 3000   Ⓒ January 1, 4000

    Ⓑ January 1, 3001   Ⓓ January 1, 4001

7. Which of these words has three consecutive sets of double letters?

    Ⓐ bookkeeper   Ⓒ pizzazz

    Ⓑ committee   Ⓓ Mississippi

8. In Source 1, the reporter has asked some people to spell *millennium*. Which answer shows the number of people who spelled the word correctly?

    Ⓐ 1 out of every 4   Ⓒ 1 out of every 12

    Ⓑ 1 out of every 6   Ⓓ 1 out of every 24

Part 3: Search "Double the Fun!" to find one example of each of the following. Then write the number of the source in which you located this information.

9. word meaning "general agreement" _____ Source #: _____

10. word meaning "a highly learned person" _____ Source #: _____

Double the Fun! *(cont.)*

Name: _____

Part 4: Refer back to the sources, and use complete sentences to answer questions #12 and #13.

11. Source 3 contains 12 words that have at least two sets of double letters within them. Write the 12 words in the order they appear.

    1st. _____

    2nd. _____

    3rd. _____

    4th. _____

    5th. _____

    6th. _____

    7th. _____

    8th. _____

    9th. _____

    10th. _____

    11th. _____

    12th. _____

12. In Source 1, there is disagreement over when a new millennium begins. With which side of the debate do you agree? State your preference and make a case for why you are correct.

_____

_____

_____

_____

_____

_____

13. Write a short paragraph that contains at least four words that contain two sets of double letters. Do this without using any of the words from Source 3. Your paragraph can be about any subject.

_____

_____

_____

_____

_____

_____

_____

_____

The Pet-Store Thief

Read each source below. Then complete the activities on pages 80–81.

Source 1

"Good morning, Ladies and Gentlemen of the jury. Throughout the course of this trial, I will prove that my client, Ian Gage, is innocent of the charges against him. You will hear from several witnesses who can vouch for Mr. Gage's whereabouts at the time these crimes were committed in May of last year. They will verify that he was not within five miles of any of the Paw's Pets when they were robbed.

"I will introduce police reports that will show that, in all four robberies, the thief gained access into the Paw's Pets stores through vents and small windows. Please look at Mr. Gage and decide for yourselves if he is physically capable of that. In addition, locks were picked on each store's cash register. Mr. Gage's physician will testify that a painful medical condition has robbed my client's fingers of the ability to perform such a nimble task.

"Lastly, Mr. Gage will be called to the stand. You will see that he is a fine citizen with no prior criminal record. In fact, he is a pet lover who often purchased items from a local Paw's Pets! His well-trained parrot, Houdini, is a beloved companion. If the court allowed, I would call that highly intelligent creature to the stand, as he could attest to Mr. Gage's caring nature.

"In conclusion, I ask that you listen closely and judge fairly. Mr. Gage is not the thief he is accused of being."

Source 2

PAWTUCKET POLICE REPORT

MAY 7, 2019

SUMMARY: This is the fourth robbery in the last four nights. Paw's Pets (three separate locations) has been the target in each case. In all four robberies, the thief stole four bills (totaling exactly $42) from the cash register. In addition, each store's display of birdcages was knocked over, and several cages were destroyed.

Source 3

Exhibit C

```
PAW'S PETS
Customer Receipt

March 9, 2019

Bird snacks       $4
Silver cage      $42
Feeder            $3
_____
Total         $49.00

Signed x___Ian Gage___
```

Source 4

Glossary of Terms

defendant — in a court case, the person accused of committing a crime

modus operandi — Often shortened to *M.O.*, this Latin phrase means "method of operation." A criminal's *M.O.* is his/her way of committing a crime.

suspect — person suspected of committing a crime

The Pet-Store Thief *(cont.)*

Name: _____

Part 1: Read each idea. Which source gives you this information? Fill in the correct bubble for each source.
(Note: More than one bubble may be filled in for each idea.)

Information Sources ➡	1	2	3	4
1. Mr. Gage bought items at Paw's Pets.	○	○	○	○
2. Houdini is a parrot owned by Mr. Gage.	○	○	○	○
3. Paw's Pets was robbed four times.	○	○	○	○
4. Mr. Gage's first name is Ian.	○	○	○	○

Part 2: Fill in the bubble next to the best answer to each question.

5. Judging by how it is used in Source 1, what is another word for *physician*?

   Ⓐ judge   Ⓒ doctor

   Ⓑ lawyer   Ⓓ defendant

6. From the information in Source 1, we know that Mr. Gage is a _____.

   Ⓐ suspect   Ⓒ pet owner

   Ⓑ defendant   Ⓓ *all of the above*

7. Provided the information we are given, which of these statements is not true?

   Ⓐ One Paw's Pets store was robbed twice in four days.

   Ⓑ Mr. Gage bought a bird feeder on March 9, 2019.

   Ⓒ The total money stolen in the four robberies was $168.

   Ⓓ Mr. Gage's trial is taking place in the year 2019.

8. Which of the following is **not** part of the pet-store thief's *M.O.*?

   Ⓐ taking $50 from the register   Ⓒ knocking over cages

   Ⓑ entering through a vent   Ⓓ picking the lock on the register

Part 3: Search "The Pet-Store Thief" to find one example of each of the following. Then write the number of the source in which you located this information.

9. two-word phrase meaning "very smart" _____   Source #: _____

10. two-word phrase meaning "cherished friend" _____   Source #: _____

Part 4: Refer back to the sources, and use complete sentences to answer these questions.

11. In Source 2, we learn that the thief always steals from the cash register four bills equaling an exact amount. Which four bills would the thief have to steal in order to get this amount?

12. In the space below, summarize the defense strategy of Mr. Gage's lawyer/attorney. Use your own words. Give a brief description of the important evidence the attorney will use to show that Mr. Gage did not commit the robberies.

_____

_____

_____

_____

_____

_____

13. Based on the evidence given in Sources 1, 2, and 3, do you think Mr. Gage committed the crimes? If not, who might have done it? Give evidence and reasons to support your opinion.

_____

_____

_____

_____

_____

_____

The Four Applicants

Read each source below and on page 83. Then complete the activities on pages 84–85.

Wanted: The Right Set of Eyes!

Company: iRis Media

Location: Arcadia, CA

Hours: Part-Time (20 hrs. per week)

iRis Media

Job Description:

Are you a prolific reader who has an eye for detail? Do you know the difference between a colon and a semicolon? Are you the type of person who, in a nice way, corrects your friends when they say things like "You and me are smart" or "I write good"? Do you find yourself catching every spelling error on the menu whenever you go to a restaurant? And finally, do you enjoy laughing?

If you leapt out of your chair and shouted, "That's me!" to any or all of these questions, then we have the perfect opportunity for you. iRis Media is a new Web-based company that specializes in online humor. Everything that we print is hilarious (at least we think so)! Our publications include books, magazines, newspapers, and comic books; and we are looking for a brilliant enthusiastic individual with amazing people skills and the ability to find a needle in a haystack (or a missing comma in a 40-word sentence).

Candidates should meet the following requirements:

* ✳ College degree in English, journalism, or other related field.

* ✳ Ability to work under tight deadlines.

* ✳ Ability to work well with others.

* ✳ Excellent computer skills.

* ✳ Flexible hours.

Pay starts at $12 per hour. If you wish to apply for this position, send an e-mail to **jobs@iRis.com**. Please type "Job Applicant" in the Subject line of your e-mail.

In the body of your e-mail, briefly describe your experience and tell us why you would be a good fit for our company. If we are interested, we will then request a copy of your résumé.

Source 2

From   patpratt@catinahat.com

Subject   HIRE ME

Wow I'd be perfect for this job!!! I am the funnyest guy I know! Also I have very good grammer, and I can read really good. I have a degree in english so I must be smart. LOL! All of my friends say that I'm easy to get along with. When do I start?

– Patrick P.

Source 3

From   highIQ@singular.com

Subject   Job Applicant

To Whom It May Concern,

I am supremely qualified for this position. I am a voracious reader with impeccable grammar, and I have yet to make a spelling mistake in the last 11 years of life. While other candidates may be under consideration, my accomplishments are redoubtable. Without much effort, I earned a degree in English from a prestigious university. I am disciplined, detailed, and highly intelligent. In short, I have always been the most impressive person I know. I will lift up your company, and my co-workers will have no choice but to improve their performance if they wish to remain employed. While your job posting was cute and charming, it was riddled with errors. Thus, you must already know that your company is in dire need of my services.

Reply promptly so we can discuss salary.

Most respectfully,
Ivan Quinn

Source 4

From   bwest@byline.com

Subject   Job Applicant

Hello, iRis Media. My name is Ben West, and I believe I would be a good fit for your company. Reading and laughing are two of my favorite pastimes! As a writer and editor for my high school newspaper, I learned the value of teamwork and of meeting deadlines. In college, I worked my way up to Senior Editor by the time I graduated with a degree in journalism. I also write a blog and edit a successful online magazine.

I would welcome the chance to meet with you to discuss this opportunity and to see if I can become a member of your team.

Thank you,
Ben West

Source 5

From   ace006@quicknet.com

Subject   Job Applicant

Hey, Iris Media. I'm writing to tell you that I could do this job in my sleep! I've been reading since I was an infant. Seriously, it's not rocket science.

HAHAHA, JUST KIDDING!!!!! See, I'm funny. What else am I? I am a good reader who will catch every error you can throw at me. I've been to school and all that, and my last boss said I was nice. I've attached my résumé, so you can see that I've had a lot of jobs. People keep hiring me, so I must be a good worker!

Let me know,
-Ace Evans

The Four Applicants (cont.)

Name: _____

Part 1: Read each idea. Which source gives you this information? Fill in the correct bubble for each source. (Note: More than one bubble may be filled in for each idea.)

Information	Sources ➡	2	3	4	5
1. This person has a degree in Journalism.		○	○	○	○
2. This person has a degree in English.		○	○	○	○
3. This person spells *grammar* incorrectly.		○	○	○	○
4. This person tries to make jokes and use humor.		○	○	○	○

Part 2: Fill in the bubble next to the best answer to each question.

5. Which applicant used incorrect capitalization to write the name of the company in his e-mail?

Ⓐ Ace Evans   Ⓒ Ivan Quinn

Ⓑ Ben West   Ⓓ Patrick Pratt

6. If the person hired works 20 hours per week at the starting rate, how much would he or she earn in one week?

Ⓐ $120   Ⓑ $200   Ⓒ $220   Ⓓ $240

7. The applicant in Source 3 uses several large words. Judging by how these words are used, which can you infer means "extremely serious or urgent"?

Ⓐ voracious   Ⓑ impeccable   Ⓒ dire   Ⓓ redoubtable

8. In Source 1, the second paragraph ends with a 40-word sentence that is missing a comma. Where should a comma be added to make the grammar correct?

Ⓐ "a brilliant, enthusiastic individual with amazing people skills"

Ⓑ "a brilliant enthusiastic individual, with amazing people skills"

Ⓒ "with amazing people skills, and the ability to find"

Ⓓ "or a missing comma, in a 40-word sentence"

Part 3: Search "The Four Applicants" to find one example of each of the following. Then write the number of the source in which you located this information.

9. word meaning "activities done for enjoyment" _____   Source #: _____

10. word meaning "a record of experience" _____   Source #: _____

Name: _____

Part 4: Refer back to the sources, and use complete sentences to answer these questions.

11. The applicant in Source 2 makes many errors. In the space below, rewrite the body of his e-mail. Use his words, but correct any misspellings and add any needed punctuation. Underline each correction.

_____

_____

_____

_____

12. Of the four, which applicant should iRis Media hire? _____

Give two reasons why this applicant could be a valuable asset to the company. Give one reason—along with supporting evidence—why each of the other three applicants would not be good hires for the company.

_____

_____

_____

_____

_____

_____

_____

13. Write a paragraph to iRis Media explaining why you should be considered for the job. For the purposes of this exercise, pretend that you have already earned a college degree.

_____

_____

_____

_____

_____

_____

_____

_____

Making Money

Read each source below and on page 87. Then complete the activities on pages 88–89.

Source 1

Glossary of Currency Terms

circulation – the movement and exchange of money in a country

currency – system of money used in a country

E pluribus unum – Latin phrase ("out of many, one") featured on U.S. currency

mint – a place where money is coined

numismatology– the study or collection of coins or other currency

seigniorage (*seen yer ij*) – the difference between the value of money and the cost to produce and distribute it

---

Source 2

THE NUMISMATOLOGY NEWS

January 2, 1999   *"Keeping Current on Currency since 1911"*

U.S. EYES SHINY NEW PROFITS

by Larry Moore

The U.S. Mint has found a new way to make money: by making money. Yesterday, Delaware's quarter became the first coin released under the 50 States Quarters program. And it's set to make more money than it's worth.

How can that be? It's all about *seigniorage*. This fancy French word describes the profit made when a coin's value is worth more than the cost of producing it. For example, it only costs 5¢ to make and distribute each new quarter. The value of each quarter is 25¢. This results in 20¢ of profit. And this profit is really expected to grow as a result of our coin-collecting hobby. The hope is that we numismatologists (another fancy word) will seek out the new quarters and keep them. We won't spend them. By doing this, we will be taking the quarters out of circulation.

This will mean that more new quarters need to be made by the Mint—and bought by the public—at a profit of 20¢ per quarter. Over the 10-year program, this will produce about $3 billion in *seigniorage* for the federal government.

The 50 quarters will be released from 1999–2008. Five quarters will be released each year. The quarters will be released in the order in which the states joined the Union, beginning with Delaware (the 1st state) yesterday and ending with Hawaii in late 2008. After Delaware, the following state quarters will be released in 1999: Pennsylvania (on March 8), New Jersey (May 17), Georgia (July 19), and Connecticut (October 12). Each quarter's design will feature the state's motto and will depict important events, objects, or people from the state's past.

Source 3

The design for the back of the coins in the 50 States Quarters program:

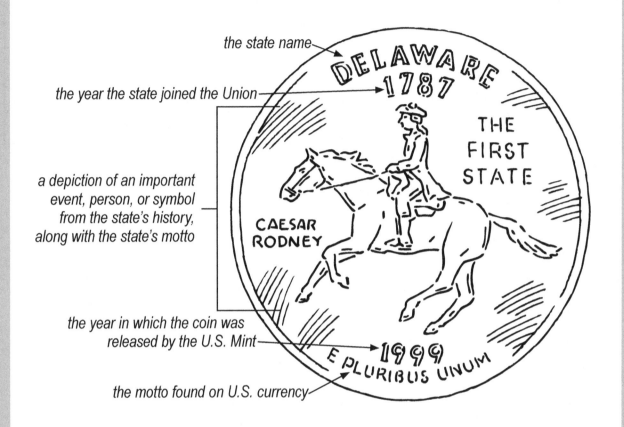

the state name

the year the state joined the Union

a depiction of an important
event, person, or symbol
from the state's history,
along with the state's motto

the year in which the coin was
released by the U.S. Mint

the motto found on U.S. currency

DELAWARE
1787
THE
FIRST
STATE
CAESAR
RODNEY
1999
E PLURIBUS UNUM

Source 4

My report today is on Caesar Rodney, a great American patriot. Rodney was born in Delaware in 1728, and he spent much of his life defending and serving Delaware. Rodney was a high-ranking officer in the Delaware military during the American Revolution, and he served in the Continental Congress. On July 1, 1776, it was his vote that broke a tie in favor of seeking independence from Britain. In order to cast that vote, Rodney had to ride a horse 70 miles through a thunderstorm—an event that is memorialized on the back of Delaware's state quarter. Three days later, the Declaration of Independence was approved. Rodney is one of the 56 patriots who signed that famous document.

Caesar Rodney also served as President of the State of Delaware from 1778–1781. He died in 1784 in the state in which he was born.

Making Money *(cont.)*

Name: _____

Part 1: Read each idea. Which source gives you this information? Fill in the correct bubble for each source. (Note: More than one bubble may be filled in for each idea.)

Information	Sources ➡	1	2	3	4
1. Coins are made in a mint.		○	○	○	○
2. Georgia's state quarter was released in 1999.		○	○	○	○
3. "*E pluribus unum*" is written on U.S. coins.		○	○	○	○
4. Caesar Rodney is featured on Delaware's quarter.		○	○	○	○

Part 2: Fill in the bubble next to the best answer to each question.

5. Which is not an example of a motto?

Ⓐ "*E pluribus unum*"

Ⓑ "The First State"

Ⓒ "U.S. Eyes Shiny New Profits"

Ⓓ "Keeping Current on Currency since 1911"

6. Who is the primary audience for the newspaper article in Source 2?

Ⓐ the U.S. government

Ⓑ the people of Delaware

Ⓒ coin collectors

Ⓓ Larry Moore

7. A sandwich costs $5.25. You hand the cashier a $5 bill and a quarter. The next customer also buys food and receives your quarter back as change. That customer uses that quarter to buy a gumball. The owner of the gumball machine spends the quarter buying more gumballs. The quarter's journey is an example of _____.

Ⓐ seigniorage

Ⓑ numismatology

Ⓒ profit

Ⓓ circulation

8. According to the information given, which equation shows the amount of profit the federal government makes on one set of 50 quarters?

Ⓐ $50 \times 5¢ = \$2.50$

Ⓑ $50 \times 20¢ = \$10.00$

Ⓒ $50 \times 25¢ = \$12.50$

Ⓓ $50 \times 25¢ = \$75.00$

Part 3: Search "Making Money" to find one example of each of the following. Then write the number of the source in which you located this information.

9. name of the 50th state to join the Union _____ Source #: _____

10. name of the 3rd state to join the Union _____ Source #: _____

Making Money *(cont.)*

Name: _____

Part 4: Refer back to the sources, and use complete sentences to answer questions #11 and #12.

11. Was Caesar Rodney alive when Delaware joined the Union? Provide facts from the sources to support your answer.

_____

_____

_____

_____

_____

12. The title of this unit is "Making Money." What two meanings does that title have with regard to the 50 State Quarters program?

_____

_____

_____

_____

_____

_____

13. Listed below are six states. Beside each is the rank showing when the state joined the Union. Use the information provided in Source 2 to find the year in which the state's quarter was released by the U.S. Mint. The first two have been done for you.

State Name	Joined Union	Quarter Released
Delaware	1st	1999
Maryland	7th	2000
Virginia	12th	
Illinois	21st	
Oregon	33rd	
Idaho	43rd	

Mean's Many Meanings

Read each source below. Then complete the activities on pages 91–92.

Source 1

Your homework today will be to learn about three common kinds of mathematical measures we can find when we have a group of numbers. These three measures are **mean**, **median**, and **mode**.

Let's use this group of numbers:

$$2 \quad 2 \quad 3 \quad 6 \quad 7$$

➡ To find the **mean**, we add up the numbers (2 + 2 + 3 + 6 + 7 = 20) and divide the result by how many numbers there are. Since there are five numbers, we calculate 20 ÷ 5 = 4. **The mean of this group is 4.**

➡ To find the **median**, we put the numbers in numerical order and find the one that falls in the exact middle. **In this case, the median is 3.**

➡ To find the **mode**, we look to see if a number occurs in the group more often than any other number. In this group, there are two 2s and only one of each of the other numbers. **The mode of this group is 2.**

Source 2	**Source 3**	**Source 4**
mean	**mean**	**mean**
as a noun	as a verb	as an adjective

Source 2

mean
`as a noun`

1. mathematical average

   "The team's *mean* score last season was 21."

2. (with *s*) wealth

   "As a man of *means*, he could afford a luxury home."

3. (with *s*) method

   "I used all *means* available to get home before noon."

Source 3

mean
`as a verb`

1. denote

   "That word can *mean* many things."

2. signify

   "That one ant can *mean* hundreds more are on their way."

3. intend

   "I *mean* to do well on tomorrow's test."

Source 4

mean
`as an adjective`

1. cruel

   "The *mean* man won't let us play."

2. skillful

   "Mia plays a *mean* game of chess."

3. contemptible

   "Winning by cheating made his victory a *mean* feat."

Mean's Many Meanings *(cont.)*

Name: _____

Part 1: Read each idea. Which source gives you this information? Fill in the correct bubble for each source. (Note: More than one bubble may be filled in for each idea.)

Information	Sources ➡	1	2	3	4
1. A person of means has wealth.		○	○	○	○
2. The word *mean* can be a mathematical term.		○	○	○	○
3. *Mean* can be used as a synonym for "skillful."		○	○	○	○
4. *Meaning* to do something is *intending* to do it.		○	○	○	○

Part 2: Fill in the bubble next to the best answer to each question.

5. You have the following set of numbers: 3, 4, 13, 20, 20. What is the mean of this set?

Ⓐ 4   Ⓒ 13

Ⓑ 12   Ⓓ 20

6. Look again at the set of numbers for question #5. What is the mode of that set?

Ⓐ 4   Ⓒ 13

Ⓑ 12   Ⓓ 20

7. In the following sentence, which part of speech is the underlined word: "Did Max mean to be so <u>mean</u> to my mother?"

Ⓐ adjective   Ⓒ verb

Ⓑ adverb   Ⓓ noun

8. Which of the following sentences does not use *means* as a noun?

Ⓐ "Despite your modest means, you bought a boat?"

Ⓑ "This means war!" roared the excitable coach.

Ⓒ "By all means necessary, we should visit Gramps."

Ⓓ "I found the ways and means to improve my grades."

Part 3: Search "*Mean*'s Many Meanings" to find the following. Then write the number of the source in which you located this information.

9. the greatest number (in numerical form) _____   Source #: _____

10. the greatest number (in written form) _____   Source #: _____

Mean's Many Meanings *(cont.)*

Name: _____

Part 4: Refer back to the sources, and use complete sentences (when appropriate) to answer these questions.

11. Think of a **group of five numbers** that satisfy these rules:

Rule 1 — The mean, median, and mode of the group all equal 4.

Rule 2 — Only two of the numbers can be the same.

Rule 3 — No number can be larger than 7.

Write your five numbers in numerical order here: _____ _____ _____ _____ _____

12. The word *median* also has multiple meanings and usages. Look at the picture of the road below. One of the labeled areas (**1**, **2**, **3**, or **4**) is called a median. Using what you learned from Source 1, make an educated guess as to which one is the median. Explain your answer.

_____

_____

_____

_____

_____

_____

_____

13. In the space below, write a paragraph that uses the word *mean* as many times and in as many ways as possible. Incorporate at least six different meanings of *mean* into your paragraph.

_____

_____

_____

_____

_____

_____

_____

Mr. Yee's Mysteries

Read each source below. Then complete the activities on pages 94–95.

Source 1

Mr. Yee said, "Class, I am going to give you a few clues to help you solve the Mystery of the Day. For today's mystery, I am thinking of a letter of the alphabet."

"Is it a *K*?" shouted Kayla.

"Is it an *A*?" blurted Keith.

"No," laughed Mr. Yee, "It is neither an *A* nor a *K*. Though it can be a vowel, just like the letter *A*. Oh, and it can be a consonant, just like the letter *K*."

"How can it be both?" asked Annie.

"Ahh, it sounds like you have uncovered a clue. This letter can be a vowel *or* a consonant, depending on how it is used in a word. Now I will give you another clue, in the form of an analogy. Here it is: *the letter B is to second as my mystery letter is to penultimate*."

"That doesn't help," groaned Albert. "I don't what that word means!"

Mr. Yee repeated the word, "Penultimate? Let's see, what could *penultimate* mean? Let me think of other penultimate things. Well, November is the penultimate month on the calendar. And Alaska was the penultimate state to join the United States. To put that next-to-last clue into the form of an analogy: *February* is to *second* as *November* is to *penultimate*."

The class just stared at Mr. Yee.

"Hmm," he chuckled, "It looks like we have another mystery to solve: the mysterious meaning of the word *penultimate*."

Source 2

State Facts

(The numbers listed in parentheses show Alaska's rank out of the 50 states.)

Population: 710,231* (47th)

Land Area: 663,267 sq. mi. (1st)

Joined U.S.: January 3, 1959 (49th)

Capital City: Juneau

Largest City: Anchorage

* *as of 2010*

Source 3

Amy checked Clark's homework. As usual, her little brother got every answer right. Tonight, his assignment was to look at a list of words and circle the one that didn't fit in with the others. His teacher also asked him to underline every letter that functioned as a vowel in the list of words.

H<u>O</u>W	WH<u>O</u>
WH<u>A</u>T	WH<u>Y</u>
WH<u>E</u>N	(YOU)
WH<u>E</u>R<u>E</u>	

Mr. Yee's Mysteries *(cont.)*

Name: _____

Part 1: Read each idea. Which source gives you this information? Fill in the correct bubble for each source. (Note: More than one bubble may be filled in for each idea.)

Information	Sources ➡	1	2	3
1. The capital of Alaska is Juneau.		○	○	○
2. The letter *K* is a consonant.		○	○	○
3. The letter *A* is a vowel.		○	○	○
4. Amy is Clark's sister.		○	○	○

Part 2: Fill in the bubble next to the best answer to each question.

5. Which of Mr. Yee's students shouted "A!"?

    Ⓐ Keith   Ⓑ Kayla   Ⓒ Amy   Ⓓ Albert

6. In Source 3, why did Clark circle the word *YOU*?

    Ⓐ It does not begin with a *WH*.   Ⓒ It begins with a vowel.

    Ⓑ It is not a question word.   Ⓓ It is last on the list.

7. Which of these statements is true?

    Ⓐ The largest city in Alaska is also its capital city.

    Ⓑ Alaska is one of the largest U.S. states, but it is the least populated.

    Ⓒ Alaska is the largest U.S. state, but it is one of the least populated.

    Ⓓ In 2010, about 7 million people lived in Alaska.

8. Which of these analogies is **not** correct?

    Ⓐ *Juneau* is to *Alaska* as *Washington, D.C.* is to *United States*

    Ⓑ the *letter A* is to *first* as *the letter B* is to *second*

    Ⓒ *Mr. Yee* is to *teacher* as *Kayla* is to *student*

    Ⓓ *November* is to *month* as *February* is to *second*

Part 3: Search "Mr. Yee's Mysteries" to find one example of each of the following. Then write the number of the source in which you located this information.

9. a hyphenated word _____ Source #: _____

10. word with more than one *y* in it _____ Source #: _____

Mr. Yee's Mysteries *(cont.)*

Name: _____

Part 4: Refer back to the sources, and use complete sentences to answer these questions.

11. Mr. Yee's mystery letter is one that can be used as both a vowel and a consonant. Which letter can be both of these things?

[ ]

Explain your answer. In your answer, give one example of the letter being used as a consonant and another example of the letter being used as a vowel.

_____

_____

_____

_____

12. Use your answer to the above question to fill in the Venn diagram below. In the **Consonants** section, write all of the letters of the alphabet that can be used only as consonants. In the **Vowels** section, write all of the letters that can be used only as vowels. In the **Both** section, write the one letter that can be used as either a consonant or a vowel.

Consonants   **Vowels**

Both

13. What do "November," "Alaska," and the mystery letter have in common? Use this to decipher the meaning of the word *penultimate*. What does the word mean?

_____

_____

_____

_____

_____

Two Sets of Directions

Read each source below and on page 97. Then complete the activities on pages 98–99.

Source 1

A **compass rose** is a figure on a map that shows directions. An 8-point compass rose shows the cardinal directions, as well as the intermediate directions.

cardinal directions

- north (N)
- east (E)
- south (S)
- west (W)

intermediate directions

- northeast (NE)
- southeast (SE)
- northwest (NW)
- southwest (SW)

Source 2

"Hi, Timmy! This is Aunt Judy calling. You're probably still on the airplane, so I'll just leave a message. I've got directions to your Cousin Sara's graduation ceremony tonight. It's at Hillside High.

"Well, I hear that you'll be staying at the Pine Log Inn. Great choice! They take care of all of our out-of-town guests. So just turn right out of Pine Log parking lot. Next, you'll want to make a left at the third street. I think it starts with an *A*. That street winds around and takes you up a big hill until you come to a fork in the road. Take the road to the right—I can't remember what it's called. That'll take you to Oro. I remember that the name *oro* means 'gold' in Spanish. Turn right, and you're almost there! There's a little street on the left just as you pass the city library. Make a left, and then a quick right. Sara's school is at the end of that street. Oh, Tim, she's so grown up! Can't wait to see you! I'll be the one crying and clutching a box of tissues."

Source 3

"Tim, it's Uncle Rex. Your Aunt Judy said she gave you directions for Friday. Between you and me, she doesn't know a compass rose from a flower in the garden, so it's Uncle-Rex-to-the-rescue time. Alright, I'll make it easy on you. Head south on Pine as you leave your hotel. In about a $\frac{1}{2}$ mile, you'll hit a T intersection. That's Arbor. Go east. That'll get you to Norte. Follow that to the north, but *stay in the right lane*. You're gonna end up on Este, which is an east-west street. When you hit Oro Boulevard, head south for $\frac{3}{4}$ of a mile. Next, you'll need to go east on Arc Lane. If you hit Plata, you've gone too far. You can't miss Hillside from there.

Now, if I were you, I'd park in the school's southwest lot. The ceremony starts at 5:00 sharp, but you'll want to get there early. Don't be one of those stragglers who gets caught up in last-minute traffic. They announce the graduates in alphabetical order, so you know Sara's name will be one of the first ones called. Ok, see you soon, champ."

Two Sets of Directions *(cont.)*

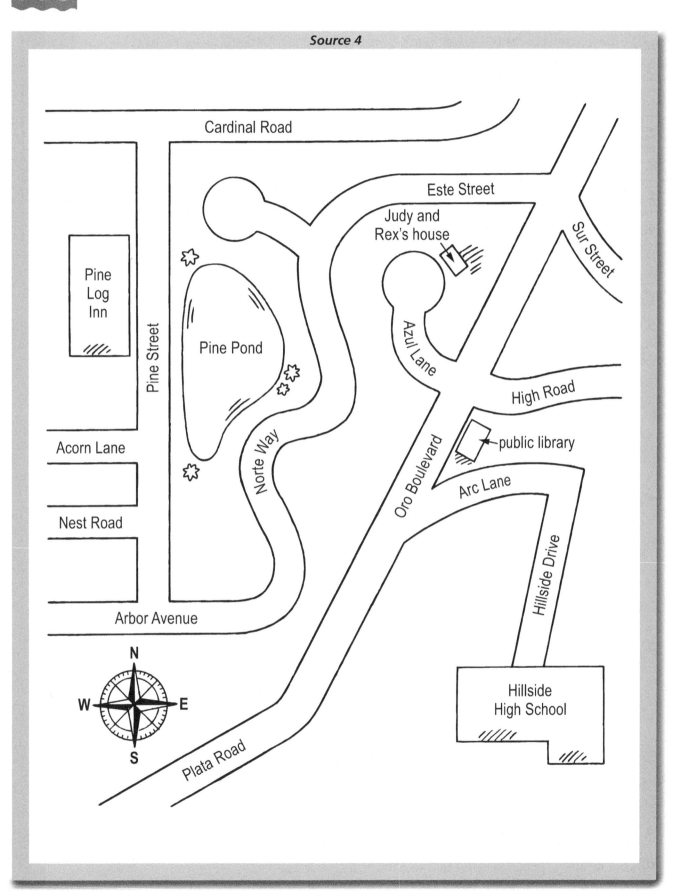

Two Sets of Directions (cont.)

Name: _____

Part 1: Read each idea. Which source gives you this information? Fill in the correct bubble for each source. (Note: More than one bubble may be filled in for each idea.)

Information Sources ➡	1	2	3	4
1. Tim has an aunt named Judy.	○	○	○	○
2. Tim has an uncle named Rex.	○	○	○	○
3. Cardinal Road is north of Arbor Avenue.	○	○	○	○
4. There are four cardinal directions.	○	○	○	○

Part 2: Fill in the bubble next to the best answer to each question.

5. Which is not a synonym of *cardinal* as it is used in Source 1.

    Ⓐ "main"   Ⓒ "secondary"

    Ⓑ "primary"   Ⓓ "principal"

6. What can be said about Uncle Rex in comparison to Aunt Judy?

    Ⓐ He lives closer to Hillside High.   Ⓒ He is more proud of Sara.

    Ⓑ He is more emotional.   Ⓓ He is more detail-oriented.

7. From the information provided, what can we infer about Tim's cousin Sara?

    Ⓐ She gets good grades in school.

    Ⓑ She has stayed at the Pine Log Inn.

    Ⓒ Her last name starts with an *A* or *B*.

    Ⓓ She has never flown on an airplane.

8. If the intersection of Pine and Arbor is a T intersection, then which of these intersections is also a T intersection?

    Ⓐ Pine and Cardinal   Ⓒ Este and Oro

    Ⓑ Oro and Plata   Ⓓ Arbor and Norte

Part 3: Search "Two Sets of Directions" to find one example of each of the following. Then write the number of the source in which you located this information.

    9. word meaning "grasping" or "clenching" _____ Source #: _____

    10. word meaning "people who are slow to arrive" _____ Source #: _____

Two Sets of Directions *(cont.)*

Name: _____

Part 4: Refer back to the sources, and use complete sentences to answer these questions.

11. Whose directions were easier to follow, Aunt Judy's or Uncle Rex's? Explain your reasons for feeling this way. (There are no right or wrong answers!)

_____

_____

_____

_____

_____

_____

_____

_____

12. Find Pine Pond on the Source 4 map. Use at least two cardinal directions and two intermediate directions to describe where it is in relation to other places on the map (Pine Log Inn, Hillside High School, Cardinal Road, etc.).

_____

_____

_____

_____

_____

_____

13. Find Aunt Judy and Uncle Rex's house. In four steps, give directions from their house to Hillside High School. Use the following in your directions:

▶ street names ▶ cardinal directions ▶ transitional words (*First, Next, Then*, etc.)

Step 1 _____

Step 2 _____

Step 3 _____

Step 4 _____

Additional Activities

1. Now that you have read all of the sources for this unit, do you see any connections between them? What do they have in common? Write up to four connections. (Note: Some units may have fewer.)

_____   _____

_____   _____

Now go back and rank the connections you have just written. Which one seems to be the strongest or most important to the overall unit? Write a "1" next to the strongest connection, a "2" next to the second-strongest, etc.

2. Fill in the chart below to show the elements that describe each source. You may fill in as many bubbles as are appropriate. (Note: Some rows will be left blank if there are fewer than five sources in the unit.)

Source # Element ➡	fiction	nonfiction	chart	map	graph	diagram
Source 1	○	○	○	○	○	○
Source 2	○	○	○	○	○	○
Source 3	○	○	○	○	○	○
Source 4	○	○	○	○	○	○
Source 5	○	○	○	○	○	○

3. It's your turn to be a teacher. Write a new multiple-choice question based on the reading sources. Then provide four answer choices, only one of which is correct. If possible, make your "students" dig a little deeper to find the correct answer to your question. Don't make your question one whose answer is written directly in the text.

Your Question: _____

_____

Ⓐ _____   Ⓒ _____

Ⓑ _____   Ⓓ _____

4. Once again, imagine that you are the teacher. Think of two words, phrases, numbers, etc., that your students will need to search the sources to find. For example, give the definition of a word, and have everyone find that word. Name a part of speech and ask for an example. Challenge your "students" to find a word with a certain number of syllables. There are many possibilities.

Search for _____

Search for _____

Answer Key

Unit 1. Aaron's Errands (page 6)
Part 1
1. Sources 1 and 2
2. Sources 1 and 2
3. Source 1
4. Sources 1 and 3

Part 2
5. B and C
6. B
7. C
8. A

Part 3
The source number is given in parentheses.
9. "you were sleeping like a log" (1)
10. Ariel's (1, 2), sister's (1)

Part 4
11. Yes, it was. The total from Party World was $37.89, and the total from Foodland was $58.01. This means that the total cost was $95.90 ($37.89 + $58.01 = $95.90). Aaron would have $4.10 left over, because $100 − $95.90 = $4.10.
12. Aaron is Ariel's older brother. We know from Source 1 that Aaron is old enough to drive a car. We also know that Ariel is having a themed birthday party with mermaids, which probably means she's younger. Also, their mom refers to Ariel's "little friends."
13. No, he did not. The time on the Foodland receipt says 1:13 p.m., while the time on the Party World receipt reads 2:00 p.m. on the same day. This means that he shopped for groceries before shopping for party decorations.

Bonus: Accept appropriate responses. Students might mention that Aaron was buying several items—such as ice and ice cream—that would need to be kept very cold. So, it would be wiser to shop for decorations first and buy the food last.

Unit 2. The Naming of the Storm (page 9)
Part 1
1. Source 3
2. Sources 2 and 3
3. Sources 1, 2, and 3
4. Source 3

Part 2
5. D
6. B
7. D
8. A

Part 3
The source number is given in parentheses.
9. alphabetical (3)
10. evacuate (1)

Part 4
11. Hurricane season seems to take place in late summer. In Sources 2 and 3, we are given several examples of devastating hurricanes, all of which took place in August through October. Of the options given, these months most closely fall in the season of "late summer."
12. Accept appropriate responses.
13. Students should supply one name for each letter of the alphabet, with the exceptions of Q, U, X, Y, and Z. They should not use any of the hurricane names mentioned in the sources.

Unit 3. Written Without Ease (page 12)
Part 1
1. Sources 1 and 3
2. Source 1
3. Source 2
4. Source 3

Part 2
5. A
6. C
7. B
8. C

Part 3
The source number is given in parentheses.
9. mayor (1), author (1)
10. English (1, 3), American (1), Greek (2)

Part 4
11. Instead of "Written Without Ease," the title could have been "Written Without *E*s." This is because "ease" and "*es*" are homophones, and both titles would be true of the novel called *Gadsby*. It was difficult to write, and the letter *e* never appears in it.
12. Accept appropriate responses.
13.

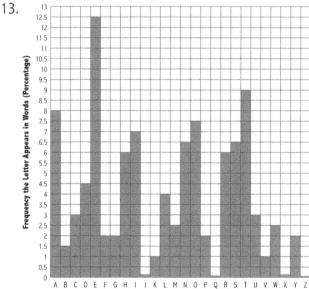

Unit 4. An Eponymous Comet (page 16)
Part 1
1. Source 4
2. Source 3
3. Source 2
4. Sources 1 and 3

Answer Key *(cont.)*

Part 2

5. A   6. D   7. C   8. A

Part 3

The source number is given in parentheses.

9. noun (3), adjective (3)

10. green (4), silver (4)

Part 4

11. Mark Twain was born (or "came in") on November 30, 1835, which was just two weeks after Halley's Comet reached its perihelion. Twain died on April 21, 1910, which was the day after Halley's returned and reached its perihelion. Twain's prediction was accurate, as he "went out" while Halley's Comet was passing by Earth.

12. Halley's Comet is an eponymous comet in that it is named after a person. Source 1 tells us that Edmond Halley calculated the orbit of this comet and also lent his name to it. Source 3 tells us that an object named after a person is called an *eponym*.

13. Accept appropriate responses.

Unit 5. #34 for 34 *(page 19)*

Part 1

1. Sources 1 and 2   3. Sources 1 and 3
2. Source 1   4. Source 3

Part 2

5. D   6. B   7. C   8. C

Part 3

The source number is given in parentheses.

9. lbs. (3), RB (3)

10. "as graceful as a ballerina" (1), "like it was a toothpick" (1)

Part 4

11. The first one is the exaggeration. Joe uses this exaggeration to prove his point about Bo Jackson. He can't believe that a 250-pound person could run up a fence like Bo did. However, we know from Bo's football card (Source 3) that he weighed 227 pounds, not 250.

12. The title ("#34 for 34") refers to Bo Jackson's last run as a professional football player. The first "34" refers to the jersey number he wore as a running back for the Los Angeles Raiders (as shown in Source 3). The second "34" refers to the length in yards of Bo Jackson's final carry as a professional football player (as stated in Source 1).

13. Accept reasonable responses.

Unit 6. Many Ways to Convey *(page 22)*

Part 1

1. Source 3   3. Source 1
2. Source 2

Part 2

4. B   5. D   6. D   7. B   8. A

Part 3

The source number is given in parentheses.

9. time-travel (3), e-mail (2)

10. piping-hot (3)

Part 4

11.

	Slice A +	Slice B +	Slice C +	Slice D +	Slice E
Cost Per Slice	$4.00	$1.50	$2.50	$2.50	$1.50
				Total Cost	$12.00

12. Accept appropriate responses. The definition given should be something along the lines of "to carry from one place to another." The explanation can be that all three sources talk about carrying something (a message, a person, a slice of pizza) from one place to another.

13. Accept appropriate responses.

Unit 7. At the Top, Looking Down *(page 26)*

Part 1

1. Source 3   3. Sources 2 and 4
2. Source 2   4. Source 1

Part 2

5. B   6. B   7. A   8. A

Part 3

The source number is given in parentheses.

9. herbivore (2)   10. predators (2)

Part 4

11. An apex predator is the top predator in its food chain. It is not hunted by any other animals that live in its habitat. We can infer this by combining the definition of *apex* (from Source 1) with the information given in Source 2 by Mr. Cross. This is confirmed by the use of the term in the chart in Source 4 and by the diagram shown in Source 3.

12. The two different ways the title is appropriate for a hawk are as follows: 1. As the apex predator of its habitat, it is at the "top" of its food chain looking down (see the diagram in Source 3). 2. A hawk

Answer Key *(cont.)*

hunts from the sky. It looks down on its prey before swooping down to attack it.

13. Accept reasonable responses.

Unit 8. In the Blink of an Eye *(page 29)*

Part 1
1. Source 4
2. Source 2
3. Source 1
4. Source 4

Part 2
5. A   6. C   7. B   8. C

Part 3
The source number is given in parentheses.
9. milliseconds (2)   10. briefest (2)

Part 4
11. You could take the data for how often the average person blinks in 60 minutes (one hour) and multiply that by 24, since there are 24 hours in a day. You would take the result and multiply it by 7, since there seven days in a week. This is would tell you how often the average person blinks in one week.

12. 1. It keeps your eyes from drying out. 2. It removes dust and other objects from eyes. 3. It helps refocus your brain.

13. Less blinking dries out your eyes, allows more objects to collect on the surface of your eyeballs, and it deprives your brain of resetting itself as frequently. This information is given in Source 2. From Source 4, we can see that a computer user blinks less than half as often as the average person not using a computer. For example, in 10 minutes, a computer user blinks about 70 times, as opposed to the non-user, who blinks about 150 times.

Unit 9. The Fourth Time's the Charm *(page 32)*

Part 1
1. Sources 1, 2, 3, and 4
2. Sources 3 and 4
3. Source 4
4. Sources 3 and 4

Part 2
5. C   6. A and C   7. A   8. C

Part 3
The source number is given in parentheses.
9. definitely (3)   10. accommodate (1)

Part 4
11. A. Athens, Paris, Los Angeles; B. London

12. No Olympic Games were held during the XII and XIII Olympiads. These Games would have been held in 1940 and 1944. This information is provided in Source 4, where we see that no Games are listed for those Olympiads. In Source 2, we learn that the Games were not held during World War II, which took place between 1939–1945.

13. A. "the third time's the charm"; B. This means that if something fails the first two times it's tried, it might still succeed on the third try; C. The saying "the fourth time's the charm" applies to Rio de Janeiro because the city tried three times previously to host the Olympic Games. It failed on those three occasions (1936, 2004, 2012), but succeeded the fourth time it tried (2016).

Unit 10. February 29, 2100 *(page 36)*

Part 1

	Year	Divisible by 4?	Divisible by 100?	Divisible by 400?	Leap Year?
1.	2000	Yes	Yes	Yes	Yes
2.	2200	Yes	Yes	No	No
3.	3000	Yes	Yes	No	No
4.	4444	Yes	No	No	Yes

Part 2
5. C   6. C   7. A   8. D

Part 3
The source number is given in parentheses.
9. 365.2425 (2)   10. divisible (2)

Part 4
11. The answer is "in the future, in the Southern Hemisphere." We know the story takes place in the future because the narrator says, "Today is February 1, 2100." We know Zeet's family lives in the Southern Hemisphere because they went to the beach on February 29, 2096, which was "a warm, summer day." According to Source 3, February is a summer month in the Southern Hemisphere.

Answer Key *(cont.)*

12. The calendar was not defective. There will not be a February 29th in the year 2100. On the Gregorian calendar, there are no leap days in years that are exactly divisible by 100 (which 2100 is) unless they are also exactly divisible by 400 (which 2100 is not).

13. Yes. Answers will vary.

Unit 11. Baking Badly (page 39)

Part 1

1. Source 1
2. Sources 2 and 4
3. Source 2
4. Sources 2 and 3

Part 2

5. D   6. A   7. B   8. B

Part 3

The source number is given in parentheses.

9. inedible (3)   10. contestant (3)

Part 4

11. Accept reasonable responses. The best example of hyperbole in Source 3 might be the statement, "It was the worst thing anyone has ever eaten." Students should explain that this is hyperbole because it is a greatly exaggerated claim. As bad as the brownies were, they could not have been the worst thing that has ever been eaten in the history of mankind.

12. Dee's brownies were awful because she used way too much salt. The recipe in Source 1 calls for $\frac{1}{4}$ of a teaspoon of salt, but in Dee's *mise en place* (Source 4), we can see that she used $\frac{1}{4}$ of a cup of salt. This may explain why they tasted like "sweaty gym socks dipped in chocolate."

13. Accept appropriate responses. Students should draw the ingredients and the equipment needed to make a breakfast food. For example, if the chosen food was cereal, students might draw a cereal box, milk, a bowl, and a spoon.

Unit 12. The Winning Whiskers (page 42)

Part 1

1. Source 2
2. Source 4
3. Sources 1, 2, and 3
4. Source 3

Part 2

5. D   6. A   7. C   8. B

Part 3

The source number is given in parentheses.

9. 1,855,993 (4); 1,381,944 (4)
10. Dear Sir (1), My dear little Miss (2)

Part 4

11. "if I was a man I would vote for you"

12. A. Electoral. B. Popular. You can tell this is true because the pie chart on the left shows a section (labeled Lincoln) that is larger than half of the pie. The only number in the Source 4 chart that is over 50% is Lincoln's electoral vote (59.4%). Also, Douglas had a much larger percentage of the popular vote than he did of the electoral vote. His section is much larger in the circle on the right.

13. Accept reasonable responses. A student might say that Lincoln's beard did help him win because it set him apart from the other candidates, none of whom had beards, judging from the pictures in Source 4. However, it would be more accurate to say that there is not enough information provided to make the determination that Lincoln's beard had anything to do with the election results. In fact, his beard would have been nowhere near fully grown on November 6, the day of the election.

Unit 13. Friggatriskaidekaphobia! (page 46)

Part 1

1. Source 2
2. Source 3
3. Sources 1 and 4
4. Sources 1 and 3

Part 2

5. C   6. A   7. B   8. D

Part 3

The source number is given in parentheses.

9. 31313 (1)   10. RSVP'd (3)

Part 4

11. March 13, 2013. From the invitation (Source 1), we know that the party is on March 13, 2026. We also know that she is turning 13 ("Our little Eve is officially becoming a teenager!"). From Source 4, we know the meaning of the term "golden birthday," which tells us that Eve is turning 13 on the 13th. Students might also mention that Eve's e-mail address contains the number "31313", which could stand for her birth date (3/13/13).

Answer Key *(cont.)*

12. The oldest one can be on a golden birthday is 31, because that is the most days a month can have.
13. Accept responses that show an understanding of the term "golden birthday."

Unit 14. **Everything Floats** (page 49)
Part 1
1. Source 2
2. Source 2
3. Source 1
4. Source 1
Part 2
5. D   6. D   7. B   8. C
Part 3
The source number is given in parentheses.
9. lounging (1)   10. microscopic (1)
Part 4
11. It is called the Dead Sea because most things cannot live in it. Large aquatic animals like fish can't live there, and neither can aquatic plants.
12. Each section represents 5%. Students should shade in seven sections, which would equal 35%.
13. From the other sources, we have learned that objects float in very salty water. Using this knowledge, we can deduce that Jim must have added a lot of salt to the red cup when Nick wasn't looking. The egg didn't float in the blue cup because the water did not contain enough salt (or any salt).

Unit 15. **Just Deserts** (page 52)
Part 1
1. Sources 2 and 3
2. Source 2
3. Sources 2 and 3
4. Sources 2 and 4
Part 2
5. C   6. C   7. B   8. A
Part 3
The source number is given in parentheses.
9. converts (4)   10. desserts (1)
Part 4
11. It would be most correct to say that the idiom applies to both Sam and Todd. For Sam, the term "just deserts" means "reward." Her reward for being well prepared is that she enjoys the experience of walking through the desert. For Todd, the term "just deserts" means punishment. He is punished for not taking the trip seriously enough and not preparing

for the harsh desert environment. For failing to do this, his punishment is a miserable experience.
12. "The sun beats down on you like an angry insect that you cannot swat away."
13. Students might also label the eyes (third eyelid keeps sand out), nose (nostrils close to keep sand out), coat (thick to protect against sand), hump (contains fat that converts to water).

Unit 16. **The Unneeded Earmuffs** (page 56)
Part 1
1. Sources 2 and 3
2. Source 3
3. Sources 1 and 4
4. Source 3
Part 2
5. C   6. C   7. B   8. A
Part 3
The source number is given in parentheses.
9. thermometer (3)   10. international (1)
Part 4
11. Mr. Shirk seems to prefer the Celsius scale. We can infer this when he stresses that "the rest of the world, along with the *entire* scientific community" uses the Celsius scale. After giving the freezing and boiling temperatures for the Celsius scale, he says, "Now isn't that easier to remember?"
12. The earmuffs are unnecessary because Alicante is extremely warm at this time. We can guess from the time of year (August) and the information provided in Sources 3 and 4 that Maria means the temperature is 35°C. Using the converter in Source 2, this means that it's about 95°F. That's several degrees warmer than the average August temperature in Alicante. Juan should be packing hot-weather clothing.
13. Accept appropriate responses.

Unit 17. **A Fallible Friend** (page 59)
Part 1
1. Sources 1 and 3
2. Source 2
3. Source 2
4. Source 1
Part 2
5. E   6. A   7. A   8. B

Answer Key *(cont.)*

Part 3

The source number is given in parentheses.

9. misused (1)   10. inexact (2)

Part 4

11. *Infallible* means "perfect" or "does not make mistakes." This definition is indirectly given in Source 1. Since we learn in Source 2 that the prefix *in-* means "not," we can deduce that *fallible* means "not perfect" or "capable of making mistakes."

12. fore, for; piece, peace; Theirs, There's; cot, caught

13. Accept appropriate responses.

Unit 18. Pioneers in Space *(page 62)*

Part 1

1. Source 2   3. Source 1
2. Sources 2 and 3   4. Source 2

Part 2

5. D   6. A   7. D   8. B

Part 3

The source number is given in parentheses.

9. two decades (3)   10. feat (3)

Part 4

11. Students should point out that Andrew referred to Soviet space travelers as "astronauts." The correct term is "cosmonauts."

12. Accept appropriate responses.

13.

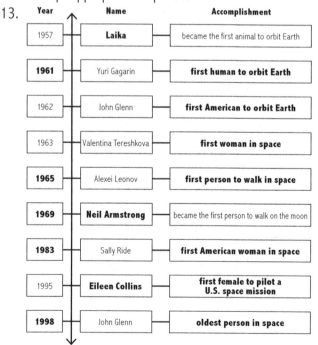

Year	Name	Accomplishment
1957	**Laika**	became the first animal to orbit Earth
1961	Yuri Gagarin	**first human to orbit Earth**
1962	John Glenn	**first American to orbit Earth**
1963	Valentina Tereshkova	**first woman in space**
1965	Alexei Leonov	**first person to walk in space**
1969	**Neil Armstrong**	became the first person to walk on the moon
1983	Sally Ride	**first American woman in space**
1995	**Eileen Collins**	**first female to pilot a U.S. space mission**
1998	John Glenn	**oldest person in space**

Unit 19. A Grain of Salt *(page 66)*

Part 1

1. Source 4   3. Sources 2, 3, and 5
2. Sources 3 and 4   4. Sources 2, 3, and 4

Part 2

5. C   6. D   7. D   8. A

Part 3

The source number is given in parentheses.

9. *the* (2)   10. FOREVER (3)

Part 4

11. Vick Z. Accept appropriate rewrites that contain complete sentences and proper grammar.

12. Todd Pepper. He owns a competing restaurant, and this would likely affect his opinion. He stands to profit from taking business away from Grain of Salt.

13. A. Foodie

Unit 20. Winning Isn't Everything *(page 69)*

Part 1

1. Source 4   3. Source 2
2. Source 5   4. Source 4

Part 2

5. D   6. A   7. B   8. B

Part 3

The source number is given in parentheses.

9. capsizing (4)   10. sacrificed (4)

Part 4

11. Accept appropriate responses in which students accurately rewrite one of the quotes, paraphrase the chosen quote, and then give an example of it from everyday life.

12. Most likely, students will choose the quote from Source 2. Lemieux did not win his race, but his heroic actions saved two of his fellow sailors.

13. Accept appropriate responses.

Unit 21. Two One-of-a-Kinds *(page 72)*

Part 1

1. Mole and Platypus   3. Mole
2. Platypus   4. Neither

Part 2

5. C   7. A
6. B (44 teeth, 22 appendages)   8. B

Answer Key *(cont.)*

Part 3
The source number is given in parentheses.

9. retracts (3)   10. consume (2)

Part 4

11. Accept appropriate responses.

12. Accept appropriate responses. Each student should use evidence from the sources to construct a persuasive argument that shows why the chosen animal is more unique than the other animal.

13. Accept appropriate responses. Students should write two essays, each from the perspective of a different animal. Each animal should explain why it believes it best represents the chosen category. (For example, if the category is "Most Dangerous," students may choose to write essays from the perspectives of sharks, mosquitos, snakes, etc.)

Unit 22. Double the Fun! *(page 76)*

Part 1

1. Source 2   3. Source 1
2. Source 1   4. Source 2

Part 2

5. A   6. B   7. A   8. B

Part 3

The source number is given in parentheses.

9. consensus (1)   10. scholar (1)

Part 4

11. 1st: raccoon, 2nd: coffee, 3rd: dumbbells, 4th: bookkeeper, 5th: mattress, 6th: Mississippi, 7th: access, 8th: committee, 9th: occurred, 10th: pizzazz, 11th: hiccupped, 12th: embarrassing

12. Accept appropriate responses.

13. Accept responses that include at least four words with multiple double-letter combinations, none of which are duplicates from Source 3.

Unit 23. The Pet-Store Thief *(page 79)*

Part 1

1. Sources 1 and 3   3. Sources 1 and 2
2. Source 1   4. Sources 1 and 3

Part 2

5. C   6. D   7. D   8. A

Part 3

The source number is given in parentheses.

9. highly intelligent (1)
10. beloved companion (1)

Part 4

11. The thief always steals $42, so students should fill in the bills with two $20s and two $1s (or a $20, two $10s, and a $2).

12. Accept appropriate responses that are written in the students' words and contain evidence from Source 1 (e.g., Mr. Gage has an alibi, he is physically incapable of committing the crime, he has no prior record).

13. Accept appropriate responses that are supported by evidence.

Unit 24. The Four Applicants *(page 82)*

Part 1

1. Source 4   3. Source 2
2. Sources 2 and 3   4. Sources 2 and 5

Part 2

5. A   6. D   7. C   8. A

Part 3

The source number is given in parentheses.

9. pastimes (4)   10. résumé (1, 5)

Part 4

11. <u>Wow,</u> I'd be perfect for this job! I am the <u>funniest</u> guy I know! <u>Also,</u> I have very good <u>grammar,</u> and I can read really <u>well.</u> I have a degree in <u>English,</u> so I must be smart. LOL! All of my friends say that I'm easy to get along with. When do I start?

12. Accept appropriate responses that follow the directions given.

13. Accept appropriate responses.

Unit 25. Making Money *(page 86)*

Part 1

1. Sources 1, 2, and 3   3. Sources 1 and 3
2. Source 2   4. Sources 3 and 4

Part 2

5. C   6. C   7. D   8. B

Part 3

The source number is given in parentheses.

9. Hawaii (2)   10. New Jersey (2)

Answer Key *(cont.)*

Part 4

11. Caesar Rodney was not alive when Delaware joined the Union. We know from Source 4 that Rodney died in 1784. We know from Source 3 that Delaware joined the Union in 1787.

12. The first meaning is that the U.S. Mint made money when they produced and released the new quarters for the 50 State Quarters program. The second meaning is that the federal government of the U.S. made money due to seigniorage. In other words, it cost much less for the government to produce and distribute the money (5¢ each) than the value they received for the money (25¢ each).

13. Virginia – 2001, Illinois – 2003, Oregon – 2005, Idaho – 2007

Unit 26. *Mean*'s Many Meanings *(page 90)*
Part 1
1. Source 2
2. Sources 1 and 2
3. Source 4
4. Source 3

Part 2
5. B
6. D
7. A
8. B

Part 3
The source number is given in parentheses.
9. 21 (2)
10. hundreds (3)

Part 4
11. There are two possible answers: 2, 3, 4, 4, 7 *or* 1, 4, 4, 5, 6.

12. The area labeled "3" is the median. It is located in the middle of the road, and we know from Source 1 that the median is the middle number in a group of numbers. Students might also mention that *median* sounds like *medium*, which is usually the middle size between small and large.

13. Accept appropriate responses. The word *mean* should be used to show at least six different meanings.

Unit 27. Mr. Yee's Mysteries *(page 93)*
Part 1
1. Source 2
2. Source 1
3. Sources 1 and 3
4. Source 3

Part 2
5. A
6. B
7. C
8. D

Part 3
The source number is given in parentheses.
9. next-to-last (1)
10. mystery (1)

Part 4
11. The letter *y* is the one letter that can be used as either a consonant or a vowel. In Source 3, the word *you* shows an example of the letter being used as a consonant. The word *why* is an example of the letter being used as a vowel.

12. Consonants: b, c, d, f, g, h, j, k l, m, n, p, q, r, s, t, v, w, x, z
    Vowels: a, e, i, o, u
    Both: y

13. All three are the next-to-last items in a series of things. November is the next-to-last month in the calendar year. Alaska was the next-to-last state to join the Union (it was the 49th out of 50), and the letter *y* is the next-to-last letter of the alphabet. The word *penultimate* means "next to last" or "second to last."

Unit 28. Two Sets of Directions *(page 96)*
Part 1
1. Sources 2 and 3
2. Source 3
3. Source 4
4. Source 1

Part 2
5. C
6. D
7. C
8. A

Part 3
The source number is given in parentheses.
9. clutching (2)
10. stragglers (3)

Part 4
11. Accept appropriate responses that choose a set of directions and make a case for why that set would be easier to follow.

12. Answers will vary. Examples of cardinal directions: Pine Pond is east of Pine Log Inn. Pine Pond is south of Cardinal Road. Examples of intermediate directions: Pine Pond is northwest of Hillside High School. Pine Pond is northeast of Acorn Lane.

13. Example of an appropriate answer: First, head southeast on Azul Lane. Next, head south on Oro Boulevard. After that, go east on Arc Lane. Finally, turn south onto Hillside Drive.

Common Core State Standards

The lessons and activities included in *Mastering Complex Text Using Multiple Reading Sources, Grade 5* meet the following Common Core State Standards. (©Copyright 2010. National Governors Association Center for Best Practices and Council of Chief State School Officers. All rights reserved.) For more information about the Common Core State Standards, go to *http://www.corestandards.org/* or visit *http://www.teachercreated.com/standards/*.

Reading: Informational Text	
Key Ideas and Details	**Units**
ELA.RI.5.1 Quote accurately from a text when explaining what the text says explicitly and when drawing inferences from the text.	1–28
ELA.RI.5.2 Determine two or more main ideas of a text and explain how they are supported by key details; summarize the text.	1–28
ELA.RI.5.3 Explain the relationships or interactions between two or more individuals, events, ideas, or concepts in a historical, scientific, or technical text based on specific information in the text.	1–28
Craft and Structure	**Units**
ELA.RI.5.4 Determine the meaning of general academic and domain-specific words and phrases in a text relevant to a *grade 5 topic or subject area*.	1–28
ELA.RI.5.5 Compare and contrast the overall structure (e.g., chronology, comparison, cause/effect, problem/solution) of events, ideas, concepts, or information in two or more texts.	1–28
ELA.RI.5.6 Analyze multiple accounts of the same event or topic, noting important similarities and differences in the point of view they represent.	4–6, 11–12, 15, 19–21, 24, 28
Integration of Knowledge and Ideas	**Units**
ELA.RI.5.7 Draw on information from multiple print or digital sources, demonstrating the ability to locate an answer to a question quickly or to solve a problem efficiently.	1–28
ELA.RI.5.8 Explain how an author uses reasons and evidence to support particular points in a text, identifying which reasons and evidence support which point(s).	21, 23
ELA.RI.5.9 Integrate information from several texts on the same topic in order to write or speak about the subject knowledgeably.	1–28
Range of Reading and Level of Text Complexity	**Units**
ELA.RI.5.10 By the end of the year, read and comprehend informational texts, including history/social studies, science, and technical texts, at the high end of the grades 4–5 text complexity band independently and proficiently.	1–28

Common Core State Standards *(cont.)*

Reading: Literature	
Key Ideas and Details	**Units**
ELA.RL.5.1 Quote accurately from a text when explaining what the text says explicitly and when drawing inferences from the text.	1–28
ELA.RL.5.2 Determine a theme of a story, drama, or poem from details in the text, including how characters in a story or drama respond to challenges or how the speaker in a poem reflects upon a topic; summarize the text.	1–28
ELA.RL.5.3 Compare and contrast two or more characters, settings, or events in a story or drama, drawing on specific details in the text (e.g., how characters interact).	4, 12, 20–21, 24, 28
Craft and Structure	**Units**
ELA.RL.5.4 Determine the meaning of words and phrases as they are used in a text, including figurative language such as metaphors and similes.	1–28
ELA.RL.5.6 Describe how a narrator's or speaker's point of view influences how events are described.	16, 19, 21, 23, 28
Range of Reading and Level of Text Complexity	**Units**
ELA.RL.5.10 By the end of the year, read and comprehend literature, including stories, dramas, and poetry, in the grades 4–5 text complexity band independently and proficiently.	1–28

Reading: Foundational Skills	
Phonics and Word Recognition	**Units**
ELA.RF.5.3 Know and apply grade-level phonics and word analysis skills in decoding words.	1–28
ELA.RF.5.3.A Use combined knowledge of all letter-sound correspondences, syllabication patterns, and morphology (e.g., roots and affixes) to read accurately unfamiliar multisyllabic words in context and out of context.	1–28
Fluency	**Units**
ELA.RF.5.4 Read with sufficient accuracy and fluency to support comprehension.	1–28
ELA.RF.5.4.A Read grade-level text with purpose and understanding.	1–28
ELA.RF.5.4.C Use context to confirm or self-correct word recognition and understanding, rereading as necessary.	1–28

Common Core State Standards *(cont.)*

Writing	
Text Types and Purposes	**Units**
ELA.W.5.1 Write opinion pieces on topics or texts, supporting a point of view with reasons and information.	5–7, 12, 15, 18–24, 28
ELA.W.5.2 Write informative/explanatory texts to examine a topic and convey ideas and information clearly.	1–28
ELA.W.5.3 Write narratives to develop real or imagined experiences or events using effective technique, descriptive details, and clear event sequences.	3, 6, 21, 24
Production and Distribution of Writing	**Units**
ELA.W.5.4 Produce clear and coherent writing in which the development and organization are appropriate to task, purpose, and audience. (Grade-specific expectations for writing types are defined in standards 1–3 above.)	1–28
Research to Build and Present Knowledge	**Units**
ELA.W.5.7 Conduct short research projects that use several sources to build knowledge through investigation of different aspects of a topic.	1–28
ELA.W.5.8 Recall relevant information from experiences or gather relevant information from print and digital sources; summarize or paraphrase information in notes and finished work, and provide a list of sources.	1–28
ELA.W.5.9 Draw evidence from literary or informational texts to support analysis, reflection, and research.	1–28
ELA.W.5.9.B Apply *grade 5 Reading standards* to informational texts (e.g., "Explain how an author uses reasons and evidence to support particular points in a text, identifying which reasons and evidence support which point[s]").	1–28
Range of Writing	**Units**
ELA.W.5.10 Write routinely over extended time frames (time for research, reflection, and revision) and shorter time frames (a single sitting or a day or two) for a range of discipline-specific tasks, purposes, and audiences.	1–28

Common Core State Standards *(cont.)*

Language	
Conventions of Standard English	**Units**
ELA.L.5.1 Demonstrate command of the conventions of standard English grammar and usage when writing or speaking.	1–28
ELA.L.5.2 Demonstrate command of the conventions of standard English capitalization, punctuation, and spelling when writing.	1–28
Knowledge of Language	**Units**
ELA.L.5.3 Use knowledge of language and its conventions when writing, speaking, reading, or listening.	1–28
Vocabulary Acquisition and Use	**Units**
ELA.L.5.4 Determine or clarify the meaning of unknown and multiple-meaning words and phrases based on grade 5 reading and content, choosing flexibly from a range of strategies.	1–28
ELA.L.5.4.A Use context (e.g., cause/effect relationships and comparisons in text) as a clue to the meaning of a word or phrase.	1–28
ELA.L.5.4.B Use common, grade-appropriate Greek and Latin affixes and roots as clues to the meaning of a word (e.g., *photograph, photosynthesis*).	3–4, 13, 17–18, 23
ELA.L.5.5 Demonstrate understanding of figurative language, word relationships, and nuances in word meanings.	1–28
ELA.L.5.5.A Interpret figurative language, including similes and metaphors, in context.	1–28
ELA.L.5.5.B Recognize and explain the meaning of common idioms, adages, and proverbs.	1–2, 4–6, 9, 15–16, 19–21, 24
ELA.L.5.5.C Use the relationship between particular words (e.g., synonyms, antonyms, homographs) to better understand each of the words.	1–28
ELA.L.5.6 Acquire and use accurately grade-appropriate general academic and domain-specific words and phrases, including those that signal contrast, addition, and other logical relationships (e.g., *however, although, nevertheless, similarly, moreover, in addition*).	1–28

Made in the USA
Middletown, DE
23 March 2019